CW00690226

Twice Nightly

An Illustrated History of Entertainment in Preston

DAVID HINDLE

Carnegie Publishing

Programme

All the author's royalties from the sale of this book will be shared equally
between the followng two charities:

DERIAN HOUSE CHILDREN'S HOSPICE, ASTLEY VILLAGE, CHORLEY
'Derian House is a place for living where laughter and tears fit side by side in
caring for terminally ill children'

ST CATHERINE'S HOSPICE, LOSTOCK HALL, PRESTON
'St Catherine's Hospice: providing special loving care for the people
of Preston, Chorley and South Ribble since 1985'

Copyright © David Hindle 1999

First published in 1999
by Carnegie Publishing Ltd, Chatsworth Rd, Lancaster LA1 4SL

All rights reserved.
Unauthorised duplication
contravenes existing laws

British Library Cataloguing-in-Publication data
A catalogue record for this book is available from the British Library

ISBN 1-85936-072-6

Typeset and originated by Carnegie Publishing
Printed and bound by Redwood Books, Trowbridge

Foreword

As I sat in the Golden Lion Pub aboard the Cunard *QE2* ocean liner travelling north to the Arctic, I was regaled by this friendly East Lancashire voice asking me if I was interested in theatres, especially those in the Preston area. What a question to ask a man whose idols were Norman Evans, George Formby, Frank Randle, Harry Worth, to name but four. 'I'm writing a book about them,' says the voice, 'would you write the foreword for it please?'

How delighted I was to say 'Yes!' Apart from a genuine desire to help the project, I felt that a certain David Hindle (some 30 years one of Lancashire's finest constabulary) needed help, maybe even counselling, as he faced this daunting task. Face it he did, however, and these few introductory words about those affectionate times and places only serve to entice me into the content hereafter.

Read about the wonderful Preston theatres and savour the waves of nostalgia that will engulf you. The names and faces that appeared in these venues will surprise you ... It's a 'reet good read'!

Jim Bowen

From the Hippodrome to Coronation Street

Personal Recollections of Roy Barraclough

Royal Hippodrome

This theatre had probably the strongest influence on me as a child. At the age of ten, or thereabouts, I was taken there by my parents to see a touring production of *The Desert Song*. At the interval I went down to buy an ice cream and I remember passing a door marked 'private' and wondering what went on behind it. Well, like all children of that age I just had to find out, so I pulled it open and sneaked backstage. Unlike the glamorous 'front of house' area, here was a world of scene shifters, unpainted corridors and dirt. One of the stage managers told me to clear off and I wandered back, tail between my legs, to the foyer. This encounter, this glimpse of a world completely unknown to me, fired my imagination to such an extent that later, at home, I made a model theatre from an old cardboard box and my love for the footlights was ignited.

Four years later, the Royal Hippodrome became home to the Reginald Salberg Players who performed weekly repertory theatre. By this time, I was studying at the Harris Junior Technical College and used to spend lunchtimes hanging around at the stage door trying to catch a glimpse of any activity. I had also been saving my pocket money up for some time in order to purchase a season ticket and this admitted me to a new world. Here I saw such stars of the day as John Barron, Derek Benfield, Frederick Jaeger, Jean Kent, Nancy Mansfield, Joan Peart, Leonard Rossiter and Nellie Wallace, to name but a few. To me, sitting in the fourth row of the circle every week was heaven on earth ... well, Preston, at least!

When I was sixteen, and by now an active junior member of Preston Drama Club, I actually appeared on the Hippodrome stage. It was with the Salberg Players and I played a schoolboy in a drama called The Housemaster alongside John Barron, Robert Chetwyn and Freddie Jaeger. It was not only a dream come true but also I managed to earn £4 for the week! Soon after that, the popularity of 'rep.' began to flag and various touring productions began using the theatre. Plays, which at that time were considered rather sensational, such as *Cosh Boy*, *The Respectable Prostitute*, *No Trees in the Street* and *A Girl called Sadie*, were staged there, starring among others Pat Phoenix.

My other memory of this theatre is the pantomime season. These were touring commercial productions, sometimes as many as three or four visiting Preston during one Christmas period. I used to go and see them all! I still recall the announcement that the theatre was to close. It was a dreadful blow. I felt real outrage when the building was pulled down.

The Palace

This was Preston's old variety theatre and I remember being taken by my parents to see the pantomimes and, when they felt it was all suitable, to see the variety bills. I clearly recall the speciality acts – the lady who walked the tightrope from the stage up to the gallery holding a rather faded parasol and then slid all the way back from the roof to the footlights (a most daring stunt, I thought), the man on the motorbike whirling round inside a metal globe, the man who conducted electricity through his body in order to light a bulb . . . wonderful!

Later, in my teens, Hylda Baker, Norman Evans, Jimmy James, Sandy Powell, George Robey (who I never liked), Vesta Tilley, Robb Wilton and Frank Randle (who I thought was by far the funniest comic), all appeared there. Then, just like legitimate theatre, with the advent of television variety began to die. Strip shows took their place with titles such as *Peaches and Screams*, *Who goes Bear?* and, of course, *Soldiers in Skirts*, featuring a very young Danny La Rue. Eventually the Palace was closed and pulled down too, with another loss to Preston.

The Playhouse

The home of Preston Drama Club of which I was a member alongside ladies like Susan Hanson and Mavis Rogerson. Here we provided probably the highest standard of amateur theatre to be found in the country. This was the place where I spent all my free time and where I learnt so much and became hooked on theatre which resulted in my turning professional in 1962.

Roy Barraclough

The Overture

This book examines Preston's cinema and theatre heritage, its evolution, prosperity and decline. Looking at Preston's entertainment history from the golden years of music hall to today, I hope to show the impact of social change on the industry, and to stir the memories of theatre and cinema-going people, who queued 'twice nightly' in all types of weather to see their favourite 'turns'.

Get the habit: twice nightly at the Empire. (Lancashire Library, Harris Reference Library, Preston)

In the days when the average wage was £2 0s. 0d., families had the opportunity to have a pleasant night out together and still have some money left for fish, chips, a bag of 'scraps' and a bottle of 'pop' after the show. Before World War I, the music halls were the main attraction, but as the silver screen began to have its own pulling power several of Preston's theatres were altered to enable them to show films. These were originally silent, of course, with live orchestral accompaniment until the introduction of recorded sound-on-film in the 1920s.

However, live theatre was sustained and theatrical digs were available in abundance.

The town even had its own repertory company resident at the Royal Hippodrome, but its finale came in 1957 when the curtain came down for the last time, and it was the end of the road for Preston's old theatres.

The Guild Hall entertainments complex was originally constructed for the 1972 Preston Guild, but its completion was too late for the event. Fortunately, though, the Public Hall was available for public performances in that year. I have been surprised to learn just how many legendary performers trod the boards at the Guild Hall and Charter Theatre. These include Tony Bennett, Duke Ellington, Bob Hope and Bing Crosby just prior to his sudden death in 1977. The list of performers appearing at the Public Hall and music halls is also an impressive roll call of theatrical greats.

Research and compilation has been an enjoyable and stimulating experience. It has been a privilege to share experiences whilst meeting some very interesting and helpful people who have kindly shared their fond memories. I am especially grateful to Jim Bowen for providing the Foreword, and to Prestonian, Roy Barraclough, for taking the trouble between filming schedules on ITV's *Coronation Street* to reflect on three of his beloved Preston theatres.

David Hindle

The King's Palace Theatre, Tithebarn Street, complete with performance times (on the board on the wall). (Lancashire Library, Harris Reference Library, Preston)

Prologue

'To be or not to be' – in Preston – 'that is the question'.

Did William Shakespeare stay in Lancashire at Hoghton Tower, six miles to the east of Preston and still the ancestral home of the De Hoghton family? In consideration of the question, there are certain enigmas in the surviving traces of the bard's teenage years, but overall the evidence supports the theory that he did reside there, and at other Lancashire noblemen's houses during the Renaissance.

Was Shakespeare a Catholic? Why did he use the alias William Shakeshafte, and why if Shakespeare was Shakeshafte should it have become such a secret? Significantly, had he considered the Elizabethan Court who spoke of the bloody question, 'If the Pope came to London who would you support, the Pope or the Queen?' Time to reflect again on Hamlet's famous soliloquy . . .

The Stratford/Lancashire Shakespeare link theory has been explored by Ernest Honigmann in his book *Shakespeare: the Lost Years*, and has been fully researched by Professor Richard Wilson of Lancaster University, and other leading Shakespearean academics. Indeed the theory has been described by scholars as 'the academic equivalent of striking oil', and there are ambitious plans to construct a new theatre at Hoghton Tower to stage Shakespeare's plays.

Preston was the scene of many performances by strolling players who enlivened the fairs and festivals throughout the period. Players would arrive with ceremonial fanfares and descend on inns, assembly halls and warehouses, or perform in the open air. In 1580, William's father, John, signed a pledge of faith to the English Catholics, and the presumption of William's Catholicism is no new theory. It was a Jesuit mission involving Priest Edmund Campion in the winter of 1580-81 which connected Stratford with Hoghton, and prompted William's Lancashire itinerary. William, torn between the pledge of faith and his country, left Stratford Grammar School and ventured north to the Catholic stronghold of Hoghton Tower to become a player and tutor for Alexander Hoghton. The story is supported by the discovery that John Cottom, a Stratford schoolmaster from 1579-81 belonged to the Lancashire gentry who were relatives of the Hoghtons.

Shakespeare used the alias William Shakeshafte at Hoghton whilst enjoying the charismatic company of Edmund Campion, who had travelled to Hoghton from Milan via Stratford. Shakeshafte had been a variant name used by William's grandfather, Richard, and if Shakespeare was Shakeshafte he was a member of a safe Catholic household for six months, which was in effect a secret college and centre of English Counter Reformation. Campion stayed with the Hoghtons until 15 May 1581. But, away from the relative safety of the Tower with its secret priest holes and chapel,

Campion was ambushed and arrested two months later in Berkshire, condemned for treason before being hanged, drawn and quartered at Tyburn on 1 December 1581.

It was about this time that John Shakespeare hid his spiritual testament beneath the tiles of his house and it has been an embarrassment to the Shakespeare family ever since workmen uncovered it in 1757. Cottom and Shakeshafte were legatees when Alexander Hoghton made his will on 3 August 1581. He enjoined his neighbour Sir Thomas Hesketh of Rufford Old Hall, 'to be friendly unto Fulke Gillam and William Shakeshafte now dwelling with me'.

William then discovered the wetlands of West Lancashire, where Rufford Old Hall is still situated on the edge of the once enormous marshes and lakes of Martin Mere, of which only a tiny fragment remains today. Hesketh retained Gillam but recommended William to the Stanleys, who maintained a playhouse at Knowsley, and had due affiliations with Lord Derby. Notwithstanding any conjectures of inconsistency, William joined the Queen's Wandering Players and visited other North West towns, including Knowsley, before returning to London in 1590.

It is true that there are many Shakeshaftes in Lancashire, but none had cause to lodge at Hoghton Tower, like the boy educated by recusant schoolmasters in Stratford. It is perhaps exciting to scholars that the Lancashire affiliation made Shakespeare the outstanding example of the academic heretic. The local link may have influenced themes in his writings outside the accepted cultures of Stratford and London; was it northern Catholicism that differentiated him from all who wrote for the London stage? In any event he enriched the world with his verse and drama.

Before ringing up the curtain at the Theatre Royal in Act One, here is an historical review of entertainment in Preston. I refer you to the programme for further details.

Full Circle

'Once every Preston Guild' is a local expression meaning 'once every twenty years'. It is the town's greatest indoor and outdoor extravaganza, and a book on the history of Preston's entertainment would be incomplete without reference to it. Events include the historic Guild Court, inter-denominational church and trade processions, and culminating in a Saturday night torchlight procession and varied entertainment to suit all tastes. In recent years, September Guild Weeks have attracted half a million people and the next Guild is scheduled for 2012. The Guild illustrates the progressive nature of entertainment in Preston that has been influenced by legislation, changes in technology and social attitudes.

During the seventeenth century, the stage at Hoghton Tower was set for a command performance. Entertainment fit for a king is described in Whittle's *History of Preston* and concerns the visit of King James I to Hoghton Tower in 1617. The performers of the musical ensemble were clothed in green, a favourite colour with the King, and endless was the variety with which the trumpet and the lute, the viol and the flageolet (flute), the violin and the hautboy (oboe) intermingled with harmonious result. James I ceremoniously knighted a loin of beef 'Sir Loin', whilst indulging in fine foods and beverages, an event after which the nearby public house is named.

The first reference to theatre in Preston was made by Loyalist officer Thomas Bellingham, who was with his regiment in Preston during the Civil War. On 16 August 1688, he wrote in his diary, 'Att night, I saw a farce call'd 'Ye Devil and Ye Pope'.' In annotations to his diary it is remarked that 'the farce was no doubt once played in a Preston theatre'. Charles Stuart, the Young Pretender, passed through Preston on 12 December 1745. In Whittle's *History of Preston*, it says that a band of itinerant musicians were in town on that day and they played the tune 'Hie thee Charlie home again'. In consequence of this, they were imprisoned for a while but then set free again.

The 1788 Public General Act was passed to enable Justices of the Peace to restrict theatrical performances to a space of 60 days. Permanent theatres were rare in the 18th century and embryonic music hall was becoming increasingly popular in rooms annexed to public houses. In the north of England, the Georgian Theatre, Richmond, and Grand Theatre, Lancaster, survive as two of the oldest in the country. In Lang's Map of Preston, published in 1744, the earliest theatre in Preston is shown situated in Woodcock's Court, off Fishergate. General Burgoyne was on stage here in 1771 when he spoke on behalf of the charities of Preston. This was the original Playhouse, but was quickly abandoned due to dilapidation. The class-conscious Theatre Royal was built on almost the same site and opened in 1802, and was the real birth place of theatre in the town, offering drama, opera and musical performances. At that time the

The site of Preston's first
theatre in Woodcock's
Court. (Lancashire
Library, Harris Reference
Library, Preston)

establishment of theatres and performers was under the direct control of the Crown.
Programmes were long, diverse and often puritanical, until an Act of Parliament sought
to legislate for theatre regulation throughout the country.

The 1843 Theatre Act was brought to bear at the Theatre Royal following an incident
when a youth was arrested and imprisoned. The *Preston Guardian* of 19 February 1868
reported that 'Edward Gibbons was charged with being drunk and smoking in the
Theatre Royal on Saturday last. He was locked away on account of the many complaints.
Edward Tannett, the Stage Manager, cautioned all persons against smoking as the
respectable portion of the audience had been obliged to leave the theatre the previous
evening on that account. The Mayor (from the bench) wished it to be understood that
smoking in the theatre was against the regulations. Fined one shilling or seven days in
jail.' The views of temperance and social order prevailed on a mainly bourgeois audience.

There was an increased demand for leisure and entertainment with the coming of
the railway system. The *Preston Chronicle* of 5 June 1841 reported that 'Three hundred
and fifty seven passengers were conveyed on the newly opened Preston to Longridge
Railway, with four trains despatched each way, to explore the fells and quarries of
Longridge, and the good folk of Longridge had a trip to witness the festivities of Preston
on Whit Monday. This included the Friendly Societies paraded in the morning and
the Temperance Society in the afternoon, and both with bands of music. In the thronged
streets, itinerant musicians from a blind fiddler attended only by his dog, to a complete
band of first rate performers were exerting themselves for the seekers of pleasure'.

The *Era Almanack Annual*, first published in 1869, has been scrutinised by Joyce
Knowsley for the period under review and a brief outline of her findings has been
deposited in the Harris Reference Library, Preston. The year 1867 was an unprecedented
one for Preston's civic pride, with the opening of the Guild Hall within the Town
Hall, although as an entertainment venue with a capacity of 1,000, the hall was small

Clarence Music Hall,

GRIMSHAW STREET, PRESTON.

Proprietor - - - - - HARRY HARKER.

OPEN EVERY EVENING AT 7-0, SATURDAY AT 6 O'CLOCK.

THE PLACE TO SPEND A CONVIVIAL HOUR.

Great Success of the

PRESTON HAND-BELL RINGERS,

Six in number, will play some choice selections with their beautiful Peal of 104 Silver Toned Bells.
A treat to all lovers of Music.

Terrific success of the

BROTHERS MILTON,

The best Song and Dance Artistes in Lancashire.   Come and see them.

MR. FRED EDWARDS,

THE COMIC VOCALIST.

Also your Old Friend and Favourite

MR. G. B. BROWNE,

The Author and Composer of the following great Football Song, as sung nightly by him with great success.

Song—"The North End Football Team."

The noble game of football is all the rage you'll own,
And lately in that kind of sport, Proud Preston she has shown;
That in her town, she does posses, the men I'm proud to say
Who now can play and beat some of the crack teams of the day

CHORUS
Then hurrah for the North End Football team,
To try and win the English cup they mean,
We will dance and sing with joy when they win the final tie;
Shout hurrah for the North End Football team.

We've Dewhurst on the Left Wing, and Smalley by his side,
With the Ball between them, down the field they very quickly
glide.
There's Belger in the centre, the favourite of all,
The lad that put's the shakers on the keepers of the goal.

CHORUS: Shout Hurrah, &c.

With Drummond on the Right Wing and the famous Gordon to,
In the whole United Kingdom their equals are but few,
With Russell, Wilson, Robinson, I'm sure it is a treat;
When Russell's on the Leather, with his Iudiarubber feet.

CHORUS.—Shout Hurrah, &c.

There's Duckworth at the back, his play is good none can deny
And many is the time that he's protected Billy Joy;
Led on by Ross the Captain, and all admit and say,
That Ross is now the finest back in England to day.

CHORUS.—Shout Hurrah, &c.

So let us wish them all success and coupled with it too,
Their umpire Mr Sudell, their friend so staunch and true,
Long life and luck attend their lot wherever they may be;
And may the team take good advice from one that is Jim Lee.

CHORUS.—Shout Hurrah, &c.

This Song is copyright, and the sole property of Mr. G. B. Browne.

Proprietor - HARRY HARKER. | Chairman - Mr. G. B. BROWNE. | Pianist - Mr. J. PORTER.

ADMISSION FREE.

Children in arms not admitted unless brought by someone.   Seats not guaranteed after 11 p.m.

Choice Wines, Spirits, Ales, Old Ben, &c.   Football Cigars of the Finest Brand.

Barrett and Parkinson, Printers and Stationers, 31, Church Street, Preston.

Clarence Music Hall programme, complete with the first PNE supporters' song, presented by Sidney Harker in 1935. (Lancashire Library, Harris Reference Library, Preston) and somewhat inadequate. The Corn Exchange, rebuilt as the Public Hall, Lune Street, was the largest in Lancashire when it reopened in 1882, and had a capacity of 3,500.

In 1872, the town's music halls and theatres included the Theatre Royal, presenting mainly dramatic entertainment, and the public house Concert Rooms at the George and King's Head inns, Friargate, and the Sun Inn, Main Sprit Weind. It was not until the New Gaiety Palace of Varieties was opened in 1882 that there was any significant increase in the capacity of legitimate music hall, with a total capacity of 9,000 at the venues.

Preston was an expanding industrial town with a mixed economy, and towards the end of the 1890s both working class suburbs, such as Ribbleton, and middle class, residential areas like Fulwood and Penwortham, were developed within the catchment areas of the entertainment venues, which duly expanded with the rising population, which increased from 70,000 in 1851 to 91,500 by 1881, no doubt causing some optimism amongst theatrical promoters and entrepreneurs. Leo Waddington, the proprietor of the Concert Room at the George Inn, operated a token system for admission. Following his release the young man, imprisoned for smoking at the Theatre Royal, could have gained admission to the George Inn Concert Room, with a charge for a drinks token and inclusive live entertainment including smoking and drinking.

Free and easy music hall acts were being developed in the public houses, managed by publican entrepreneurs, with a room set aside for 'the turns', which were important training grounds for performers, some of whom would graduate to higher-grade halls. On 23 November 1889 in the *Preston Guardian*, the George Inn Concert Room proclaimed itself to be 'the only music hall in town with special attractions and a concert tonight at 7.30pm'. Perhaps Prestonians did not mix entertainment with serious drinking for the George Inn was demolished in 1895 to give a clear view from Friargate of the Harris Museum and Art Gallery. H.A. Graham in 1889 argued that 'it was the mobility of the audience that distinguished music halls from theatre'.

In Preston, it was clear there was a shift from class to mass entertainment, partly to satisfy the cotton and manual workers of industrial Preston who wanted to take up their own baton, echoing the well-known song of the time 'Let's All Go to the Music Hall'. Admission was free to the Clarence Music Hall that was annexed to licensed premises in Grimshaw Street. A programme of a performance with the Preston hand-bell ringers is illustrated, which will be of interest to Preston North End fans as it included the first football supporter's song.

The music hall taverns set the foundations for the architecturally designed people's emporia, incorporating new building types and styles of presentation, with splendid curtained proscenium arches and rows of seats in the purpose-built theatres.

Theatres and music halls grew rapidly throughout the towns and cities of Great Britain and audiences flocked to them. During the late Victorian and Edwardian era, Preston would reach saturation point in terms of the choice of live entertainment venues. Touring variety acts, large-scale plays and musicals prompted commercial theatrical managements such as the Broadhead family to build large theatres steeped in period splendour. Following a rebuilding of the Theatre Royal in 1882, four more theatres were built in quick succession: the Gaiety (latterly Prince's), Tithebarn Street (1882); Royal Hippodrome, Friargate (1905); Empire, Church Street (1911); and King's Palace, Tithebarn Street (1913). Tithebarn and Church Streets, formerly 'red light' areas, became the centre of Preston's cinema and theatre land – a sort of mini provincial London West End.

As Preston became an increasingly-important town on the entertainment map, so theatres were built, some of them very quickly. Theatre 'digs' also sprang up all over the town; in the Church Street, Avenham and Frenchwood areas, warm-hearted landladies provided homely accommodation for regular artists near to the town centre theatres. An 'overflow' arrangement was agreed between land-ladies for the large numbers of chorus girls, casts of pantomime and opera companies, to make sure everyone had somewhere to

The Prince's Theatre, Tithebarn Street. (Lancashire Library, Harris Reference Library, Preston)

Hoardings show what's on in 1936. Next door, The Old Shop, Fylde Street, near the Adelphi Hotel, was supposed to have been built in a day. (Lancashire Library, Harris Reference Library, Preston)

Friargate and the Royal Hippodrome Theatre in the 1950s. (Lancashire Library, Harris Reference Library, Preston)

go for a late night supper after the show, and bed and breakfast. Artists often became personal friends of their hosts who looked after them very well, and theatre landladies were around as long as the theatres remained.

The majority of Preston's theatres had been built towards the end of the music hall boom which began in the mid-1800s and lasted to the outbreak of World War I. Thereafter, the entertainment frequently changed from variety or music hall, to drama and back again, and a growing interest in animated motion pictures created a new entertainment for the 'masses'. Three theatres changed their programming from live productions to film until their eventual demise.

A cinema newsreel & local travelogue

Following Louis Lumière's first commercial film presentation in Paris in 1895, cinema was quickly established in Europe. The travelling fairgrounds showed 'motion pictures' in tents and trailers and, in 1901, the bioscope was invented. Some of the first films to be screened in Preston excited a packed audience at the old Public Hall in December 1903. The local man who undoubtedly played a key role in the history of Preston's cinema development was Hugh Rain. He was born and brought up in the Starkie Street area and, after travelling the world as an entertainer and circus performer under the stage name of Will Onda, he returned to the town from France. There he had seen a bioscope and is credited with bringing the first one into the United Kingdom.

Fascinated by the medium he became a renowned local film-maker, showing his first films, lasting only one minute, in the Ashton area. They were of poor quality and known locally as 'penny gaffs'. He covered the Royal visit in 1913, Preston Guild 1922 and the Preston vs Blackburn F.A. Cup Final in 1926, and is regarded as the town's greatest cinema pioneer. His other claim to fame was that he opened the first Preston cinema in March 1908. Reflecting the age of sobriety, it was called the Temperance Hall and was built on North Road in 1856 with 800 seats. In an advertisement of 22 June 1908, the short films shown included *Female Highwayman*, *Gamble for a Woman*, *A Motherless Child* and *Trip to Niagara*. In 1917, the hall became The Picture Palace and adjacent was the Preston Film Exchange, Onda's first venture into film distribution.

Onda began to bring about the transition of some theatres into cinemas and introduced films to the Theatre Royal in 1911 and Prince's in 1913. He established the largest film rental company in the North West in Kinema House, Corporation Street, opposite the old entrance to the university. His prosperity meant he could own one of the first motor cars in the town, and have the Regent Ballroom, Tithebarn Street, built for his wife – which rather makes it sound like she was quite a size!

In the 1920s, he acquired a former malting house which was built by Matthew Brown in 1895, and situated at the corner of Brackenbury Street and Brackenbury Place. He converted it into the bizarre-looking Picturedrome cinema, known locally as the 'Brackie'.

A 'larger-than-life' entrepreneur, Will Onda was educated at Eton College, and his parents intended him to enter the ministry, but instead he followed a completely different career. As well as his contribution to the entertainment scene, Will Onda served on the town council from 1920, becoming an Alderman in 1935, was a Director

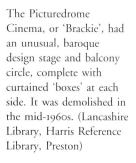

The Picturedrome Cinema, or 'Brackie', had an unusual, baroque design stage and balcony circle, complete with curtained 'boxes' at each side. It was demolished in the mid-1960s. (Lancashire Library, Harris Reference Library, Preston)

The Regent Ballroom on Tithebarn Street. (Lancashire Library, Harris Reference Library, Preston)

of Preston North End Football Club, and lived latterly at 15 Moor Park Avenue. Will Onda died in the heyday of the cinema boom in the 1940s.

After the birth of film, equally primitive and obscure cinemas, often converted from chapels and warehouses, were spawned throughout the town and its suburbs. A succession of managers tried to follow Will Onda's business ventures up to the 1930s. Will Fare from Bolton opened both the Alexander Picture House, Walker Street, near the present Salvation Army Headquarters, and the Picture Palace at the junction of Broom Street and Brook Street, which had been previously part of St Peter's School. The former became a dance hall in 1927 and the latter was showing short films including *Napoleon & Josephine* and *Curate at the Races* on 5 July 1909.

The Imperial Picture Palace, Mill Bank, Church Street opened around 1908, and was accessible through an archway opposite the prison on Stanley Street. It was originally a malt house and known to be a bit primitive. In 1928 the cinema presented *The Dangers of Ignorance*, a film open to men only about a 'serious social evil affecting the physical and mental health of the nation'. Women were enlightened on separate nights and one can only speculate about the mysterious content to be witnessed on these occasions. Coronation Hall at the corner of Waterloo Road and Wellington Road opened with a Will Onda film in 1913, the same year as the tiny Marathon Boxing Stadium & Picture Palace at 66 Frank Street. Here, disagreeing picturegoers could presumably resort to the ring for a few rounds if necessary!

Bennett's Electric Theatre on Craggs Row, off Moor Lane, was a prime example of a period cinema and was run by Ike Bennett. It was known as 'Fleckie Bennett's', a name many Preston theatregoers remember to this day. It later became the Dominion which was nicknamed 'the laugh and scratch', though the term more generally used to describe unclean and scruffy cinemas was 'fleapit'. Ike used to sit outside his cinema whilst the locals enraged him with a song about some tiny creatures:

> *Oh, ring down the curtain*
> *I can't sing tonight*
> *Those little creatures*
> *They scratch and they bite*
> *No more to the pictures will I ever go*
> *To Fleckie Bennett's in dirty Craggs Row*

Following a change of ownership, the Dominion became the Rex and until recently, it nestled in the shadow of flats on Moor Lane, close to the historic former windmill on Cragg's Row. It finally 'bowed out' when it was demolished by Norweb for industrial expansion.

During the days of silent films most cinemas had a piano or other form of live musical accompaniment. At the Star they had a trio (cello, violin and piano); the Cosy had piano and drums, in contrast to the New Victoria which on occasion had a twenty-five piece orchestra. Harold Jones was a violinist in the Palladium orchestra, which included a bass, cello, drums, trombone, trumpet, a couple of violins and the maestro on his piano. In 1992, Harold described how each Monday morning the silent film would arrive with the musical score, which was comprised of mood music that would enhance the love and dramatic scenes. On each music stand was a row of lights and appropriate music was played according to the number displayed. If the score was not supplied with the film, the musical director would decide on his own selection during the rehearsal before the mid-afternoon matinee. With the coming of 'talkies', talented musicians were made redundant, including Harold who opted for a nautical career.

The palatial Palladium, the town's first purpose-built cinema, opened on Church Street in 1915. *The Man who Stayed at Home* seemed a satirical title for the first matinee which was shown at 3.00pm and then continuously from 6.30pm to 10.30pm. The cinema was purchased by Preston Corporation in 1968 for £45,000 and was demolished to make way for a service road to the proposed Guild Hall complex.

'One-' and 'two-reelers' started to be made by film-makers in the UK and USA, and very soon Hollywood, with such screen stars as Charlie Chaplin, the Keystone Kops, Laurel and Hardy, Tom Mix and Rudolph Valentino, became well known to cinemagoers . The weekly serials, such as *Flash Gordon, The Perils of Pauline* and *Tarzan*, provided suspense and ensured subsequent visits to the local fleapit for the next week's thrilling instalment – after all, some poor woman had been left tied to a railway line in front of an advancing train, or strapped to a descending pendulum suspended over a vat of boiling oil! The old films always had scratch marks on them, giving the impression it was constantly raining.

Cinemas continued to provide local community entertainment and, during the 1920s,

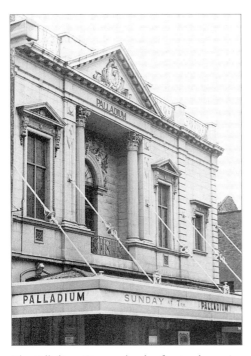

The Palladium Cinema shortly after its closure in 1968. (Courtesy of the *Lancashire Evening Post*)

began to expand significantly. The Tivoli, on Fleetwood Street near Watery Lane, opened in 1920 and had 700 seats and, when silent films were shown, there was a commentary provided by megaphone. Also the Victory (formerly a chapel and later called the Rialto), on St Paul's Road, opened on 26 April that year with 300 seats, and was described as the 'nicest and cosiest in the district'. Six years later, it had the 'latest ventilating system – cool and free from smoke', and on Fridays had a musical interlude with tenor Hamilton Bell. It closed in December 1958 with *You're in the Army Now*.

On June 6 1921, the Cosy opened in a converted chapel in St Peter's Street and was run by Alfred Wiles, a local councillor who dressed in a dapper smart blue suit and grey trilby. He was assisted by 'chucker-out' Elijah Waddilove, who maintained order with a long pole. The Cosy was the place to be on a Saturday, as locals went to the 1d. matinee, and in the evening a talent show was staged during the interval, with home-made lemonade sold in jam jars!

The Queens, Tunbridge Street, was owned by the Alderson family, and in the 1960s was called the Continental as it showed spicy films like *Paris Vice Patrol* and *Dens of Evil*. It had two rows of double seats and was renowned for its X-rated films. It will be well remembered by couples who were courting at the time, some of whom indulged in X-rated performances on the back row, whilst occasionally glancing at Brigitte Bardot starring in films billed as 'shattering, compelling and raw'!

The Lido (formerly the Grand, then the Regal) opened in 1921 and its air was blue with risqué continental films which would probably be judged benign by today's standards. One of these days I'll have to permanently repress adolescent memories of naked women walking about *The Isle of Levant* and projected onto the Lido's big screen in dazzling colour! Readers may remember the cliché displayed at London's Windmill Theatre, 'If it moves, it's rude!' The Lido, on Marsh Lane at the junction with Bow Lane, is now a car maintenance depot following its closure in November 1959. The Savoy, Ashton Street, was a purpose-built cinema, a 'cinema-de-luxe' according to the publicity, and its first film on 27 June 1921 was *The Sea Wolf*. Deluxe or otherwise, it finally succumbed to the march of progress in September 1958.

The Star, at the corner of Corporation Street and Fylde Road, also opened in 1921 and had 1,000 seats laid out in an American circular style. A supporting programme

The former Savoy Cinema, Ashton Street, in its guise as a do-it-yourself store. (Courtesy of the *Lancashire Evening Post*)

The Star Cinema, Corporation Street. (Lancashire Library, Harris Reference Library, Preston)

item in May 1927 featured 'Major Court Treatt's 12,732 mile daring motor adventure 'From Cape to Cairo'. Errol Hinds, the youngest member of the expedition, will describe the thrilling journey at each performance'. In 1929, the Star was the first to show a short supporting talkie film and was dubbed 'Preston's Talkie Theatre accompanied by our unrivalled symphony orchestra', complete with a live show consisting of a tenor, comedian and a row of dancers. It closed appropriately on American Independence Day in 1959. The Guild, Geoffrey Street, was opened for the 1922 Preston Guild, had 750 seats and remained a cinema until July 1959 when it was frozen with *Ice Cold in Alex*. Alas, it finally thawed out in October 1998 when a fire gutted the building, which was latterly used by engineering merchants.

Special performance – the New Victoria

The transition to super cinemas was accelerated in 1927 upon the arrival of the first silent film with some 'talkie' dialogue and singing: *The Jazz Singer* starring Al Jolson. The following year, Provincial Cinematograph Theatres opened their magnificent New Victoria, Fishergate, equipped with facilities for stage shows. Special features included

The New Victoria. The photograph illustrates the beautiful auditorium and orchestra pit. It is published by kind permission of Mr. D.J. Gibirdi of Preston. His grandfather had a plasterworks company on North Road and latterly Preston Fibrous Plastics in Bow Lane employed the family. The company created the ornate interior plasterwork at the New Victoria, and at the nearby Booth's grocery provision shop and upstairs cafe, which is now Waterstone's bookshop.

a spacious entrance hall and an impressive central dome in the auditorium with 1450 seats in the stalls and 670 in the circle, and a separate restaurant. The building was tastefully decorated with concealed lighting and ornate plasterwork. Reporting on the opening night of 17 September 1928 *The Lancashire Daily Post* wrote, 'with considerably more than 2,000 in the building, the atmosphere was pure and undefiled. There was a general chorus of praise for the beauty and comfort of the building and for the excellence of the entertainment'. The New Victoria epitomised the classic Art Deco cinemas of the 1920s and 30s of which there are so few left today.

A special souvenir programme produced for the opening extolled its features and the 'pictures' to be shown:

> The New Victoria is a place of high-class entertainment in which cheerfulness, good taste and comfort are happily blended. It is dedicated to lovers of wholesome amusement, to people who lead busy lives and who need relaxation. Occasionally there may be pictures of a deep human interest which will put you in a serious mood, but always there will be pictures which will grip your interest, pictures which will make you glad, will fill your soul with laughter, and will eliminate from your system the day's accumulation of household or business anxieties.
>
> The building of the theatre has been an undertaking of some magnitude. Its construction has involved the use of 1,250,000 bricks, 550 tons of cement, and 350 tons of steel. The main girder, which carries the balcony, is 75 feet in span, and weighs 30 tons. It was first intended to confine the entrance to the part of the frontage originally occupied by No. 151 Church Street but, as the work progressed, the Directors of Provincial Cinematograph Theatres decided that such a theatre deserved a more imposing front. The adjoining shop, No. 150, was therefore included making the front spacious entrance hall, and at the same time it was decided to construct a cafe on the first floor, with residential flat for the manager over.
>
> The front of the building has been treated with white 'marmola' glazed terra-cotta on simple and dignified lines. A conspicuous feature is the illuminated 'marquise' or projecting canopy. On entering the building, one is immediately struck by the air of spaciousness that runs throughout the structure. Entrance, crush hall, staircases, balcony, foyer and theatre are all planned on generous lines, and the visitor feels that whatever the number of patrons, they can all be comfortably accommodated.
>
> The stage is equipped with the well-known 'Ajax (Improved) Safety Curtain', grid, flies, etc., and there are thirteen dressing rooms, so that productions of any size can be dealt with. Heating and ventilation are on the most modern lines. The air is first filtered and washed and then warmed and dried. It is then forced into the theatre at various points without causing draughts, and is finally extracted. The quality of the fresh air thus passed through the theatre amounts to no less than two and three-quarter million cubic feet per hour. For hot weather, arrangements are made for washing and cooling the air. On

summer nights, the sliding shutters round the upper part of the dome may be lifted, giving all the advantages of a sliding roof, without the drawbacks of a possible wetting from a sudden shower.

The lighting at the New Victoria has been carried out on up-to-date lines, and embraces many novel features. Over 10,000 electric lamps, 50 miles of electric wire, and 100,000 feet of steel tubing have been used, and these simple facts alone will convey some idea of the elaborate installation necessary for the lighting of a modern theatre.

The first film shown at the New Victoria was silent with live musical accompaniment, and featured Charles Farrell in Howard Hawks' *Fazil* (USA 1928). Maestro T. S. Clarke Brown conducted an orchestra of twenty-two players, and Leslie James on the mighty Wurlitzer Organ emerged from beneath the stage during the interval. Live variety acts were the supporting programme in those days and perhaps justified the need for a large orchestra.

The opening programme included 'the first presentation in Preston of The Regent Girls with Graham and Douglas, the inseparable dancers and other high-class artists'. The most famous of the organists was Reginald Dixon, subsequently of Blackpool Tower fame, who started his career playing at the large Preston cinemas. I well remember the organ which was still in use for children's matinees in the 1950s, but it was moved from its central position when the screen was widened for Cinemascope.

Manager, Ivan Yeatman, a lieutenant during the First World War and a former manager of the Palladium Cinema, paraded the doorman and the staff before the doors opened to the public to make sure their white cardboard shirt fronts and dickie bow ties had been neatly pressed and presented, because, like the pristine new building, all the staff had to be very smart. The orchestral contingent wore red jackets, and the organist and theatre manager would emerge resplendent in best evening dress. My mother, Joan Hindle, worked in the upstairs cafe in the late 1950s and remembers the old-fashioned elegance and service that had been continuous from those early days, when 'special teas' – tea, Vienna bread and butter – sandwiches and cakes and a pot of tea were 'served on a dainty tray – available at a shilling per person'. The café remained a period piece until its closure in 1970.

A special gala was held on 26 September 1931 for *Trader Horn*, which was a very successful early Hollywood 'talkie' starring Harry Carey. The film's subject, Trader (whose real name was Alfred Aloysius Smith, which may explain why he called himself Trader!), was born in St Ignatius Square, Preston, and became an ivory and gold trader in Africa in 1880. He died in Whitstable, Kent in 1931, but one of his sisters attended the gala evening.

The heyday of the 'talkies' was enjoyed in this sumptuous and proud venue which continued in full service during World War II and had been re-named the Gaumont by 1954. Occasional live theatre was still being staged and I can recall regular visits from the Carl Rosa Opera and the Sadler's Wells Ballet. During the 1950s, highligths included *Carmen*, *La Bohème*, *Faust*, *The Rakes Progress* and other titles from the Company's repertoire. I enjoyed several productions by the Preston Musical Comedy

Society, including *Oklahoma*, and a one-night variety show featuring the comedian Harry Worth, *'My name is Harry Worth. I don't know why, but there it is!'*, and the harmonious Beverley Sisters. A Cinemascope screen was installed but, with the removal of eight rows of seats, it did not stop the stage productions taking place.

In 1962, the Rank Organisation became the owners and re-named it the Odeon, and a complete transformation of the building's structure meant it could no longer be used as a live theatre venue. In the auditorium, the circle was extended to the stage and became a 1229-seat cinema, with a dance hall called the Top Rank Ballroom (now Tokyo Jo's) constructed in the former stalls area. A modern and contemporary look meant that the magnificent dome was hidden behind acoustic tiles lined with glass wool.

At the official opening on 28 January 1963, the Rank Managing Director said 'The cinema is re-shaping itself to the needs of the 1960s. Preston is a fine example of faith in the future of the film industry'. The new manager, Bryan

The New Victoria in the early 1950s with Alistair Sim in *Scrooge*.

The Odeon/Top Rank entertainment centre, comprising a ballroom, theatre, cinema and restaurant.
(Courtesy of the *Lancashire Evening Post*)

The new Odeon Cinema closed in 1992, unable to compete with the out-of-town, multi-screen cinemas.
(Courtesy of the *Lancashire Evening Post*)

Coppock, started showing midnight films and there was great concern in January 1965 when the cinema almost 're-shaped' its patrons. The audience had left at 2.30am after watching Sean Connery as James Bond in *Goldfinger*, and at 3.00am substantial amounts of heavy plaster fell from the auditorium ceiling crushing the empty seats. James Bond was not the only one to have been 'dicing with death' that night! The ceiling was put back together again and, to the best of my knowledge, there was no reccurence of the problem.

The Odeon cinema was a forerunner of the multi-screens, with the café sacrificed to create Odeon 2 Screen in January 1970. With the boom in film-making and the attendance of famous film stars at the re-opening of the Odeon, there was great confidence in the future of cinema in 1960s Preston. But this was to prove unfounded in the 1970s as the video film hire industry, and other forms of entertainment, started to take families away from cinema going. The Odeon was in need of refurbishment and both screens ceased showing films on 12 September 1992. It was the last cinema to close in the town centre and could no longer compcte with the two multi-screen cinemas which had opened on the outskirts of the town, offering eighteen film choices, with more dynamic film and sound presentation in bright and welcoming auditoria.

The Empress

The Empress, Eldon Street, opened on 12 October 1929, had 900 luxurious seats, distinctively ruched or scalloped curtains, and was fitted with a Western Electric sound system. It was described as 'the atmospheric cinema' because during performances the frescoes were transformed with an ingenious system of changing colours. It was one of the first cinemas to have its own car park, and later in its life it showed a continuous live performance of the Queen's Coronation in 1953 before closing in the 1960s. The projection equipment must have been retained for a while because, in addition to bingo, children's Saturday matinees were shown in the early 1970s before the building was used as a roller skating rink.

The Empress Cinema on Eldon Street. (Courtesy of the *Lancashire Evening Post*)

The Carlton Cinema, Blackpool Road, Ribbleton, now a children's indoor play area. (Courtesy of the *Lancashire Evening Post*)

Tel.: 56411   GOOD SHOES AT SENSIBLE PRICES FOR ALL THE FAMILY   Est. 1911
ARTHUR GREEN and SONS   "Your Child Should Wear 'Jen' Treble Wear
"The Booteries"   : They Last for Months Without Repair" :
152, RIBBLETON LANE   FROM YOUR LOCAL 'JEN' AGENT
Preston.

SUNDAY, JUNE 10th   FOR ONE DAY

Victor Mature, Richard Egan in
GLORY BRIGADE

MONDAY, JUNE 11th   FOR THREE DAYS

—CINEMASCOPE—

Jane Russell, Jeanne Crain in
GENTLEMEN MARRY BRUNETTES
Technicolor

THURSDAY, JUNE 14th   FOR THREE DAYS

—CINEMASCOPE—

Tyrone Power, Susan Hayward in
UNTAMED
Colour by De-Luxe

SUNDAY, JUNE 17th   FOR ONE DAY

Bob Hope, Lucille Ball in
FANCY PANTS
Technicolor

BEDROOM SUITES
DINING SUITES
3-PCE SUITES
ODDMENTS
CARPETS
LINO

FREE STORAGE
FREE DELIVERY

FARNWORTH & BAMBER

184, RIBBLETON LANE,
Tel.: Preston 76395

BARGAINS FOR CASH

FITTED CARPETS
ESTIMATES FREE
SIDEBOARDS
KITCHEN CABINETS
TABLES
DIVANS
BEDDING
BEDSTEADS

A Carlton Cinema programme from 1956.

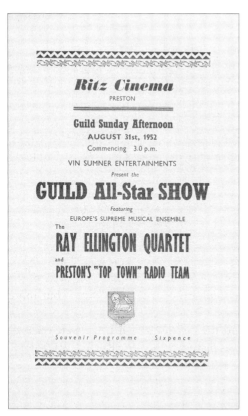

This Ritz Cinema programme from 1952 featured live entertainment for Preston Guild.

A ticket for Harry Gold and his Pieces of Eight who were on at the Queens's Hall on 9 March 1951

In the 1950s, suburban cinemas were showing three different programmes a week with 'double bills', plus Pathé News and 'trailers' for new films. This early attempt at multi-screen choice did not stop their demise, however. The Carlton, on Blackpool Road was transformed into a bingo hall on 4 November 1961, and is now a children's indoor play area. It opened on 8 August 1932 with 650 seats and was described as 'the only cinema in Preston built for 'talkies''. On 12 December, the Plaza opened in New Hall Lane with 930 seats. It was originally a cotton room and warehouse, but was transformed into a beautiful cinema with 'gilded walls of fibrous plaster, a gaily decorated stage and shaded lights with row after row of plush seats'. It was still in operation in 1964, when the screen was transferred from the closed Empire Theatre. The building can still be seen behind the petrol station next to Horrocks' Mill.

The Ritz

Hailed as the most luxurious cinema of its kind in the north, the Ritz, Church Street, was built for £45,000 and opened with George Formby in *Keep Fit* on 23 March 1937 with a new 'stadium' construction consisting of a vast raked auditorium without a balcony, with tiers on each side, containing 1650 seats and a forty-foot screen. It was the first town cinema to have a cloakroom complete with attendant, and was equipped with a stage and three dressing rooms, suggesting that limited use as a 'live venue' was anticipated. This was exploited by a young Prestonian impresario, Vin Sumner, in Guild Year 1952. On the Sunday of Guild Week, he staged a show featuring the Ray Ellington Quartet and Preston's 'Top Town' radio team. During the following week he presented another show, this time with the legendary American jazz singer, Sarah Vaughan, topping the bill.

Throughout his varied career, Vin Sumner undoubtedly played a significant part in the development of Preston's post-World War II entertainment. He started investing his own money, at both thePublic Hall and Queen's Hall, to promote the finest artists and big band sounds. In 1950, he attempted to change the perception of the Queen's Hall by introducing cabaret and calling it the Casino, with elevated areas for patrons overlooking a floor show. But this early attempt at cabaret failed after only three weeks, and he reverted back to the popular big band sounds of Harry Gold, Cyril Stapleton and many others.

In 1962, Vin started working for the Rank Organisation in Liverpool, and regularly met all the big 1960s groups, including the Beatles and their manager, Brian Epstein. Vin was appointed manager and promoter at the Top Rank Ballroom in the re-constructed Gaumont (the Odeon Cinema) in 1963. Many will remember dancing to the top groups on Wednesday nights, including Freddie & the Dreamers, The Hollies, Marmalade, The Rolling Stones and The Searchers. In the third, and last, cycle of his career, Vin was appointed supremo when the Guild Hall opened in 1972 – but more about that in Act Four, Scene Two.

The Ritz, the Palladium across the road, and the Grand, Marsh Lane, were once all owned by the Kennedy family. Bert Kennedy was pianist at both the Ritz and Palladium. The general manager at the Palladium in the 1920s, Ernie Angers (whose niece was the actress Avril Angers), went on to manage the Ritz for many years.

An enthusiastic queue of cinema-goers at the Empire, Bamber Bridge.

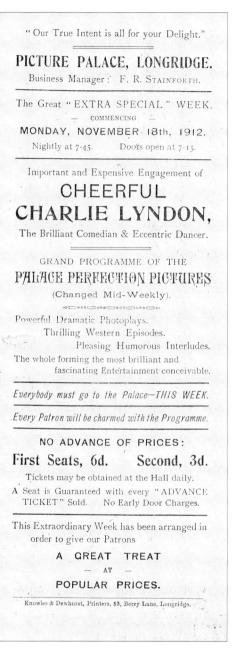

" Our True Intent is all for your Delight."

PICTURE PALACE, LONGRIDGE.

Business Manager : F. R. STAINFORTH.

The Great " EXTRA SPECIAL " WEEK,
— COMMENCING —
MONDAY, NOVEMBER 18th, 1912.

Nightly at 7·45. Doors open at 7·15.

Important and Expensive Engagement of

**CHEERFUL
CHARLIE LYNDON,**

The Brilliant Comedian & Eccentric Dancer.

GRAND PROGRAMME OF THE
PALACE PERFECTION PICTURES
(Changed Mid-Weekly).

Powerful Dramatic Photoplays.
Thrilling Western Episodes.
Pleasing Humorous Interludes.
The whole forming the most brilliant and
fascinating Entertainment conceivable.

Everybody must go to the Palace—THIS WEEK.

Every Patron will be charmed with the Programme.

NO ADVANCE OF PRICES:

First Seats, 6d.   Second, 3d.

Tickets may be obtained at the Hall daily.
A Seat is Guaranteed with every "ADVANCE
TICKET" Sold.   No Early Door Charges.

This Extraordinary Week has been arranged in
order to give our Patrons

A GREAT TREAT
— AT —
POPULAR PRICES.

Knowles & Dewhurst, Printers, 53, Berry Lane, Longridge.

In 1912, the comic Charlie Lyndon supported the Palace Perfection Pictures programme

As a youngster, I queued outside in the cold weather and slowly walked through the Ritz's long entrance foyer gazing into the window displays in anticipation of seeing *Reach for the Sky*, *The Titfield Thunderbolt*, *Treasure Island*, and other memorable films of my childhood. Born a war baby, I was too young to recall the morale boosting 'live' wartime concerts occasionally staged at the showpiece cinema. Star Holdings of Leeds took over in 1968, and Walt Henderson from the Plaza, Chorley, became manager. The canopy was dismantled, new house lights fitted, a larger screen installed, and there was much redecoration, but it still had to suffer from a change to use as a bingo hall before closure in March 1986.

Other cinemas built near Preston for the 'talkies' were the Empire, Clayton Street, Bamber Bridge (1910-58); the Lyric, Liverpool Road, Penwortham (opened on 16 March 1931 and now a garage); and, in Leyland, the Hippodrome, Preston Road (opposite Boundary Street); Palace, East Street; and the Regent, School Lane. The Hippodrome (or Green's Hippodrome) often presented live shows and had a corrugated iron sheet roof. During a rainstorm, it was impossible to carry on a conversation inside the building let alone hear the performers or film soundtrack! On hot summer nights rumour has it that the film *Cat on a Hot Tin Roof* was the favoured choice! At the Saturday afternoon children's film matinees, a one-penny entry included an orange to eat, but the performances often suffered from breakdowns and the children's outbursts were more pronounced than any rainstorm!

Until a few years ago the Palace, Longridge, continued as a lasting tribute to the old cinemas. Run by the Williamson family, it served the local community well, but sadly has now closed. It was established in 1912 as a music hall and picture palace with 375 seats, some of which were 'double seats'. There was a big door for bringing scenery in and out, and three dressing rooms still remain within the building. The cinema was operated by a gas engine as there was no mains electricity installed, and a large quarryman was the 'chucker-out'.

The closed ABC cinema, Fishergate, Preston. (Courtesy of the *Lancashire Evening Post*)

The heyday of Preston's cinemas lasted until the 1950s and 1960s. At one time there were up to twenty-two (see appendix), and all were doing a roaring trade, with post-war queues forming outside them seven days a week. Sunday screenings had been introduced during World War II with a single nightly performance, and to make sure of a seat you had to queue for at least an hour. Each of the cinemas had their own characteristics and clientele, many of whom would attend on the same weekday, week after week, irrespective of the choice of film.

Several factors led to the cinemas' demise, including television and home entertainment, as well as changing trends in entertainment which led to the conversion of many of them to bingo halls and nightclubs. In the town, the Carlton, Empire and Ritz were converted to bingo halls, never to return to showing films again. It was an end of an era too for the cheery doormen, usherettes and managers who had served

The Playhouse Theatre on Market Street West, taken during the 1940s. The home of the Preston Drama Club, the theatre is also used by many other local drama societies. (Courtesy of the *Lancashire Evening Post*)

local communities so well. No longer would they be able to welcome patrons with a warm smile and a kind word, not to mention bouts of occasional officialdom. As the audience came out of a film, the manager would shake hands with them and say, 'Av yer enjied it? See you next week!' Indeed, at the smallest cinema, patrons developed as personal a contact with the manager as with the local corner grocer. Also, the tired and worn out theatres could no longer compete and the last two, the King's Palace and Royal Hippodrome, were both empty shells awaiting their final death sentence. In later years, the historic Public Hall (Corn Exchange) in Lune Street was to be partly demolished to make way for a new inner ring road.

The ABC cinema

A late phase of cinema development occurred on 14 March 1959, when the 'ultra-modern' ABC Cinema opened on the same site as the Theatre Royal. This was the first cinema to be built in Preston after World War II and had 1400 seats. Despite an auspicious first night showing of *The Reluctant Debutante,* and the official opening filmed by Pathé News and shown around the country, the cinema was to have the distinction of being the shortest-lived major building to have been erected in the town centre. A 1973 conversion of the stalls to the Painted Wagon Public House, with an extended balcony area as a cinema, did not resolve financial losses brought about by dwindling audiences. The ABC closed on 4 September 1982 with an X-rated double bill of *The Amityville Horror* and *Phantasm,* and was demolished four years later when work started on the Fishergate Shopping Centre.

As the house lights come up, let's look at recent
local cinema and theatre innovation

The Playhouse Theatre

The 'home' of Preston Drama Club is the Playhouse Theatre, Market Street West, which started off life as a Quaker chapel in the nineteenth century before being transformed into a Knights of St Columba dance hall in about 1900. During World War II it served as a gas mask distribution centre before being purchased in 1946 by a group of dedicated amateur drama players, who became shareholders in the enterprise. The building was gutted and, after internal conversion, was re-opened as a theatre in 1949. The theatre is self-supporting with all profits going towards maintenance, and is used by the Broughton Players, the Gilbert & Sullivan Society, the Grimsargh Players, the Hoghton Players, Preston Drama Club, Schoolhouse and the Utopia Youth Theatre.

Preston Drama Club present their traditional Christmas pantomime each year, and often dig out the 'house full' signs for the capacity audience of 220, using seats salvaged from the former ABC Cinema, Fishergate. (The expression 'bums on seats' reminded me of a tale about a man who placed his hat on his seat while he went for an interval drink. He came back to find his seat occupied and indignantly said, 'That isn't fair as I put my hat on my seat to keep my place'. 'Yer did, did yer,' was the reply. 'Well, I'll tell thee summat – up 'ere, bums keep seats, not 'ats!' Ah well, such is life!)

Taking the play to the audience with a portable touring-booth theatre were the

Saul Street swimming baths, now demolished. (Courtesy of the *Lancashire Evening Post*)

travelling actors and blue-painted vehicles of Century Theatre, the UK's only mobile playhouse at that time, who visited Preston in the 1960s. It took two days and five trailers to construct the auditorium into a 225-seat venue with under-floor heating. At the time, the town was starved of professional theatre, and it provided a welcome opportunity to see a talented company in modern and classical drama. The company set up camp in Hartington Road for many years, and then in the old Starchhouse Square, presenting a world premiere of Lancaster-born playwright David Pownall's comedy *How to Grow a Guerrilla* on 25 May 1971.

David Pownall told *The Lancashire Evening Post*, 'Audiences and people generally in the North West have an unaffected directness and sincerity that you don't find elsewhere. I still don't understand why theatre was allowed to deteriorate to the condition it found itself in, in the '50s around here, but things are certainly better now'. In later years, Century Theatre took up permanent residence in Keswick. Today, many local amateur dramatic and operatic productions take place in numerous suburban halls, and there are studio theatre facilities in the university and colleges in the town where travelling professional theatre productions perform.

However, in the 1960s, there was no local theatre capable of presenting large-scale productions. The nomadic Preston Musical Comedy Society had been ousted from the

Gaumont and Empire after 1964, and in desperation turned to the local council-run swimming baths. The pool was covered with a bouncing wood floor and their first venture was the 1965 production of Franz Lehár's operetta *The Merry Widow*. Saul Street Baths, now demolished, were on the site of the Preston Crown Court complex, and will be remembered for the two outdated pools and the transformation that took place when the last of the swimmers had gone home. The water in the larger pool was drained off and the 'big plunge' was transformed into The Queen's Hall, which staged occasional performances of musical comedy, dancing, boxing and wrestling during the winter months.

The hall had never been designed as a theatre and required many adjustments by the beleagured technical members of the society, especially in relation to acoustics and lighting. At the end of the week's run, the temporary lighting grid was disassembled and the hall reverted back to baths. This drew attention to the need for a new civic theatre, and the Borough Council decided to build an entertainments complex in Lancaster Road to fulfil the function of a concert hall and theatre. The building became reality in 1972, and the Guild Hall and Charter Theatre are now firmly established. The Guild Hall superseded the old Public Hall, Lune Street, and both that and the Guild Hall are featured on the 'bill' in Act Four.

In the 1980s, a USA-inspired 'multi-screen' cinema was installed in Milton Keynes

The Queen's Hall, or Saul Street baths at night! During the winter months, when swimmers had gone home the water in the main pool was drained off and the room became a temporary theatre and ballroom, staging wrestling, boxing and occasional Preston Municipal Comedy Society productions. (Harris Museum and Art Gallery)

Ventriloquist Keith Harris is pictured at UCI, Preston, with his green-feathered duckling friend, Orville, selecting the winner of a competition to raise money for the Variety Club of Great Britain. (Courtesy of the *Lancashire Evening Post*)

to test the market for such a format. It became, and still is, very successful, with cinema-goers being offered a much wider choice of films, viewed in modern and air-conditioned venues. On one site there is everything from intimate dramas to blockbusters of *Titanic* proportions! However, the 'film experience' is different, with each screening room only having up to perhaps 300 seats, as opposed to the 2,000-seat cinemas of fifty years earlier. The atmosphere created by such large numbers of people in one place, all eagerly anticipating the latest release, cannot be matched by the multi-screen experience of today. In Preston two multi-screen cinemas have been built, with bright foyers dispensing popcorn and iced drinks, large screens, clear sound reproduction in small auditoria, and large car parks, enticing families to spend their entertainment time as easily as possible.

On Riversway in the re-claimed Preston docklands, United Cinemas International, a joint venture by American companies Paramount and Universal Pictures, opened a ten-screen cinema in March 1990. The following year, Warner Brothers opened an eight-screen cinema at the Capitol Centre, Walton-le-Dale. Both cinemas effectively closed down the Odeon Cinema in the town centre as, although Rank had considered a multi-screen cinema on that site, it was too late to decide on further development with eighteen other screens in Preston alone. The concept of building these complexes on expanding leisure and development sites with large car parks was an instant hit in the UK, and made a visit to the cinema a socially agreeable form of entertainment once again.

Proof of UCI's popularity and marketing strategy came in 1993, when the Preston venue beat twenty-nine other competing UCI-owned cinemas throughout the country. It emerged as the top UK UCI site with an average of 20,000 customers a week, and the first manager, Graham Dentith, accepted a £15,000 cheque on behalf of the cinema. Both UCI and Warner Brothers cinemas have promoted charitable events.

As we head into the twenty-first century, ABC, Rank, UCI, Warner Brothers and other cinema companies have reversed the decline of cinema for the time being. To some degree, the entertainment cycle has gone full circle, with pubs and clubs featuring comedians and music acts, just like the days of the old Clarence Music Hall, Grimshaw Street.

During the summer of 1996, a huge pop concert took place in Avenham Park and an all-girl group, the Spice Girls, sang their soon-to-be-released hit single *Wannabe*. This was their first live gig, with Queen tribute band GaGa and the Chicago Soul Band in support, and Lindisfarne topping the bill. Heralded as a great success, the two-day 'Party on the Park' attracted about 45,000 people during that July weekend, and was organised jointly by the local 97.4 Rock FM independent radio station and the Borough Council. Three years later, when my daughter told me she had seen the Spice Girls I thought she was kidding; after all who would have thought the international mega stars had started off 'down in t' park'. I have a feeling that they will not be returning their visit.

Before we get the 'show on the road' with a detailed look at the old theatres, a reminder to patrons that tea or coffee with biscuits can be reserved in the intervals. Please complete your programme slip now with your row and seat number and hand it to the usherette.

Act One, Scene One
The Theatre Royal, 1802–1955

The Theatre Royal had an illustrious history and has been described as being 'the most historic place of amusement in Preston'. In fact, the site dates back to medieval times when strolling players performed in special roped-off areas. The theatre opened coinciding with September celebrations for the 1802 Preston Guild.

A watercolour painting in the Harris Museum & Art Gallery, Preston, shows an unpretentious, small barn-like structure incorporating a loft door and hoist, with separate doors indicating 'pit', 'boxes' and 'gallery'. The theatre was fairly typical of the era and a different concept from the original music halls that were attached to public houses. It had numerous modifications made to highlight its own brand of culture and its remarkable history is written both in Hewetson's and Whittle's histories of Preston.

A body of shareholders built the theatre and had the right of free admission by transferable silver tickets. Presenting dramatic and vocal productions, it was also the

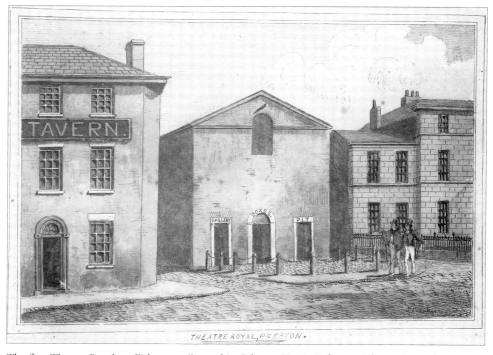

The first Theatre Royal on Fishergate. (Lancashire Library, Harris Reference Library, Preston)

This Present FRIDAY.

NEW THEATRE, PRESTON.

On FRIDAY, AUGUST 27th, 1802,

THE MUSICAL DRAMA OF THE

Mountaineers

Octavian, *Mr. SIDDONS*
Bulcazem Muley, Mr. REMINGTON
Count Virolet, Mr. BANNERMAN
Killmallock, Mr. NICHOLSON——Lope Toche, Mr. HAYES
Roque, Mr. DAWSON
Muleteers and Goatherds, Mr. NEWTON, Mr. MASON, and Mr. FROST
Sadi, Mr. CRISP

Floranthe, Mrs. H. SIDDONS
Zoriada, Mrs. CUMMINS
Agnes, Mrs. CRISP
Female Goatherds, Mrs. ROWLAND, Mrs. NICHOLSON,
Mrs. and Miss REMINGTON.

A Comic *SONG*, by *Mr. NEWTON*,
And a Favorite SONG, by Mrs. ROWLAND.

After which, a celebrated FARCE, (never performed here) called The

Wedding Day;

Or the Meeting of Old Friends.

Sir Adam Contest, Mr. CRISP
Lord Rakeland, Mr. BANNERMAN
Young Contest, Mr. MASON
Mr. Milden, Mr. FROST——John, Mr. NEWTON
Lady Contest, Mrs. CRISP
With the favorite Song of "*IN THE DEAD OF THE NIGHT.*"
Lady Autumn, Mrs. NICHOLSON
Hannah, Miss REMINGTON
Mrs. Hamford, Mrs. REMINGTON

An entire new Comic Song, called, The ASSIZES, by Mr. CRISP.

TICKETS to be had, and PLACES for the BOXES taken at Mrs. SERGENT's *(only)*
Printer, MARKET-PLACE.

BOXES 3s.....PIT 2s.....GALLERY 1s.

DOORS to be Opened at SIX, and to Begin at SEVEN o'Clock precisely.

On SATURDAY, the Tragedy of HAMLET.
Hamlet, Mr. SIDDONS.....Ophelia, Mrs. H. SIDDONS.
With LOVERS' QUARRELS.

The first Theatre Royal programme, 1802. (Courtesy of the *Lancashire Evening Post*) venue for local meetings and functions in the public and social life of the town, before the community first used the Public Hall in 1853. At the opening in 1802, legislative restrictions influenced programme structure and this typical programme shows a good balance of drama and singing. Mr and Mrs Siddons demonstrated their versatility by each playing many parts, including Sarah Siddons playing Ophelia in *Hamlet*.

A programme of 18 January 1804, informed the local public that:

> The new theatre at Preston will present the comedy "John Bull"
> For extra value "The Female Volunteer" and "The Rights of Woman"
> are to be declaimed or sung by Mrs. King
> A loyal address written and spoken by Mr. Bretherton, in character of a volunteer to the armed forces
> And "God save the King" in full chorus, followed by
> A musical exhibition of "The Turnpike Gate" with the additional song of "Miss Bailey"

The officer commanding the company of the Preston Volunteers promoted this special effort and charged high prices for those days: 3/- for a box seat, 2/- in the pit, or 1/- in the gallery.

The lengthy theatre programme usually started at 7.00pm, with cheap seats in the gallery after 9.00pm, and patrons could watch a comedy routine after the first play of the night. One such routine in 1829 involved two men, Jocko and Jacko, masquerading as monkeys and carrying out a daring escapade around the gallery and upper boxes, before eventually landing safely on the stage and delighting the audience, especially in the 'gods' (highest balcony or tier).

In 1833, Watkin Burroughs took over as Manager and, apart from redecorating the interior, he was keen 'to assure patrons that any temperance allegiance would not be prejudiced by the selling of intoxicating liquor. At a time when all classes are so earnestly exhorted to temperance, the Manager trusts it will not be irrelevant to state that a theatrical performance affords a highly rational evening's amusement and the visitor leaves the theatre frequently morally improved, and certainly without any exposure to inebriety, as no spirits or wines can be obtained even if desired'. A total abstinence pledge had originated in Preston less than twelve months before Watkin took office and he was anxious to upgrade the theatre and attract the upper strata of the social classes, for whom perfect sobriety mattered.

Marketing literature at the time stated that the interior was 'splendidly embellished' and the scenery was 'entirely repainted' in order 'to put the theatre in a proper state, to receive the first classes of society'. It was stated that the improvements had 'caused the Manager much trouble and great expense, and he therefore submits the following prices to the public and confidently trusts they will meet with general approval'. The new prices were as follows: First Price at 7 o'clock; Boxes 2s. 6d.; Pit 1s. 6d.; Gallery 6d; and Second Price at 9 o'clock: Boxes 1s. 6d.; Pit 1s. No Second Price to the Gallery.

Two of the most famous musical personalities of the nineteenth century were now set to become an important part of Preston's theatrical history. Signor Niccolò Paganini is mentioned in Whittle's *History of Preston* as giving a 'great concert in the Theatre Royal on the 27th August 1833'. Seven years later the great Hungarian-born composer and performer, Franz Liszt, trod the same boards as the virtuoso violinist when he appeared on Wednesday 2 December 1840.

The Preston Franz Liszt Recital

Liszt toured extensively in Europe and often gave concerts for charitable purposes. During 1840-41, he made further visits to England playing before Queen Victoria. In December 1840, he gave performances at five North West venues, in Halifax, Liverpool, Manchester, Rochdale and Preston. Although he would normally have received the kind of adulation now reserved for leading pop musicians, at Preston they did not even have to find the 'house full' sign.

The following review of the Preston performance appeared in *The Preston Chronicle* on Saturday 5th December 1840: 'M. Liszt's concert, under the direction of Mr. Lavenu took place at the theatre on Wednesday evening. The following was the bill of fare on the occasion:

PART ONE

1. Trio, 'Mi lagnero lacendi,' Misses Steele, Bassano and Mr. J. Parry – Mozart
2. Aria, 'L'amor suo mi fa beato,' Miss Bassano – Donizetti
3. First selection from the celebrated recitalist – pianoforte – **M. Liszt**

4. Aria, 'Che puo dirvi,' Miss Steele – Benedict

5. Prize ballad, 1840, 'Fair Daphne,' Mr. J. Parry – Parry
6. Ballad, 'Memory's Dream,' Miss Bassano – Lavenu
7. Second selection – pianoforte – **M. Liszt**
8. New duet, 'The Muleteers,' Misses Steele and Bassano – Wade
9. Mr. J. Parry will sing (by desire) his popular song, 'Wanted a Governess' – Parry
PART TWO
10. New duet, 'The Wrong Serenade,' Miss Bassano and Mr. J. Parry
11. Ballad, 'They tell me thou'rt the favoured guest,' Miss Steele – Balfe
12. Third selection – pianoforte – **M. Liszt**
13. Duet, 'The Sisters,' Misses Bassano and Steele – Wade
14. Ballad, 'I've Left a Sweet Home,' Miss Bassano
15. Fourth selection – pianoforte – **M. Liszt**
16. Song, 'The Last Adieu,' Miss Steele – Parry
17. Mr. J. Parry will sing his new song, 'A Wife Wanted' – Parry
18. Finale – ''Tis a Very Merry Thing,' Misses Steele and Bassano and Mr. J. Parry

Notwithstanding the immense merit of M. Liszt and, despite the European reputation he had so worthily acquired, the attendance on Wednesday was by no means worthy either of the musical reputation of Preston, or commensurate with his high deserts. Nevertheless, there was a fair sprinkling of the fashionables and respectables of the

In January 1856, Lady Gay Spanker featured, something which would not pass without comment today! (Courtesy of the *Lancashire Evening Post*)

town and neighbourhood, and of our numerous musical amateurs we scarcely missed a single face. It would have been gratifying, however, on such an occasion, had every part of the house been occupied to repletion; for nothing less than such an attendance could, we conceive, be remunerative to Mr. Lavenu, under whose management and engagement M. Liszt and the other 'corps musicale' are making a tour.

With regard to the performance of M. Lizst, we can truly state, that whatever expectations might have been formed of his genius, however extravagant, must have been more than realised by the execution of his four splendid concertos, embracing, as they did every variety of mechanical excellence, applied in prodigal profusion to the due rendering of the classical music, upon the selection of which M. Liszt's reputation as an artist might well be allowed to rest. His style is daring and original, not more different from the broad and simple beauty of Mendelssohn, than from the ornate richness of Thalberg.

He was heartily welcomed on making his appearance, and at the conclusion of number 3, was very loudly applauded, for he really did wonders of the most exciting and enchanting kind. In number 7, he won the hearts of all lovers of true theme, pathos and expression, by the delicate and chaste manner in which he gave one of Rossini's compositions, which was rapturously received. In numbers 12 and 15, he fully maintained the effect produced by his performance in the first part, and indeed it were next to impossible to describe the enthusiasm he excited throughout. When, however, an artist mounts beyond a certain point of excellence and of sublimate, it must be left for the imagination of better musicians than ourselves to conceive the reality; for, as in the present instance, the attempt at description on out part would be at once vain and presumptuous.'

The theatre again lived up to its 'great expectations' when Charles Dickens graced the stage during December 1861, to give readings from *A Christmas Carol* and *The Pickwick Papers* whilst on one of his frequent visits to the town. Perhaps he admired the ceiling of the auditorium that was described by another visitor that year as being 'divided into eight compartments, radiating from a sun burner in the centre with a figure disporting in each compartment. The 'boxes' over the proscenium arch, separating the stage from the audience, are hung with red curtains. They look quite as much like berths on board a ship, and the decorations generally are in

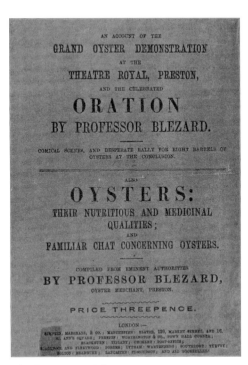

The front cover of the *Preston Mercury*, 1862. (Harris Museum and Art Gallery)

what might be called the 'paperhanging style'. The audience composed of factory operatives now occupied the 'pit' and 'gallery', and brought their babies with them.'

A Lancashire dissipation

Also that year, and in marked contrast to Charles Dickens' oration, a local charlatan, 'Professor' Robert Blezard, who was an illiterate fish merchant, trod the same hallowed boards. The gourmet Professor attempted to educate his audience in the curiosities of the deep and the wonders of the shore, and gave useful advice as to how the oyster shell might be opened and its contents devoured with aplomb. An account of the almost cataclysmic evening was documented in the *Preston Mercury*, and reflects Lancashire humour, dialect and a bygone era. The report can be found in the innermost recesses of the Harris Museum and Art Gallery basement and extracts from it are reproduced below:

The doors were opened at half-past seven o'clock, and there was a considerable rush at first into the 'gallery'. The 'house' was filled as follows: 'pit' about three-fourths, 'gallery' three-fourths, 'upper boxes' one-fourth, and 'boxes' about one-half. On taking a survey of the audience, we perceived that the fish dealing division had mustered in strong force, scarcely a member of the fraternity being absent. There were several women present. The orchestra was occupied by the Royal Sovereign Mill Band, which played through the streets up to the house. The hour fixed for commencing was eight o'clock and, from half-past seven, some jocular spirits in the 'gallery' amused themselves immensely at Mr. Blezard's expense.
We select the following from the numerous choice cries:
'Turn that owd spinner out there.'
'Be sharp, Robert, th' spinning master's coming.'
'I say Bob, is Sebastopol fortified all round?'
'Give us an antidote.' [supposed to be the lecturer's pronunciation of the word 'anecdote'.])
'Do Robert'
'Leet up th' creator.' [Mr. Blezard's pronunciation of the word 'theatre']
'There's a paddygraft (paragraph) in th' papers, Bob.'
'Blezard will be exprised to see all these fooak.'
'Where is Blezard?' Another voice, 'He's at Maude's, getting his hair curled.' Another, 'Nay, getting shampoo'd.' Another, He's getting th' three-legged stool off.' Another, 'Nay, he's getting fifteen antidotes off.'
All these sallies were followed by bursts of laughter. There was then a call for the band to play. A voice, 'Yes, play us the oyster march.' Another voice, 'Give us Blezard's galop.' The band then played a tune in splendid style, after which the vociferations of the scoffers in the 'gallery' were renewed on an extraordinary scale. Eight barrels of oysters were brought upon the stage amid great cheering

and laughter, and cries of 'Is them natives?' 'Bob's going to prostitute them?' 'He'll not allow disgussion to-neet?' 'Hez the chairman cum'd?' The audience having amused themselves in this way for some time, began to whistle, stamp and scream, and at quarter-past eight o'clock Mr. Blezard presented himself, amidst a perfect hurricane of cheers, again and again renewed.

He was dressed in a black coat, trousers and vest, with white gloves. Taking off his hat, he bowed to the assembly, and observed 'Ladies and gentlemen (laughter and cheers), I thank you for your. . .for the kind encouragement (applause) and support, and I should be very happy if this present audience (laughter) feel anxious to hear what I have to say, they will have to be very quiet (cheers and laughter). I thought within my own mind – that – that (laughter). I made up my mind that the working classes of Preston would encourage a working man (loud cheers). Therefore I shall be highly gratified if this audience will give me a fair hearing, and I must say mysel that I shall give the lecter on the – lecter on the (laughter) – on the oysters (roars of laughter) – I shall give the lecter perhaps before the evening is o'er, happen in an hour from now (great laughter).

The interval was made up of tunes from the Stanley Mills Band, songs by William Yates, "The Crinoline", "I Wish I Was Married", "Over the Hills and Far Away", "The Mon at Mestur Grundy's", and recitations by William Sandam, "God Bless these Poor Fooak". Mr. Blezard declined to present himself 'till he was ready', and many of the audience seeing the state of the case retired to the adjacent hotels. Shortly before ten o'clock, Mr. Blezard appeared on the platform, in his shirtsleeves, with an apron on, and wearing a fancy smoking cap. The theatre resounded with laughter. He certainly did not much resemble a lecturer on oysters. Perhaps if his subject had been turkey rhubarb, his dress might have been more appropriate. The 'house' speedily refilled.

Mr. Blezard advanced to the footlights with his printed lecture on oysters in his hand, and his left raised towards the 'gallery', as if to procure order. He said, 'Ladies and gentlemen, you will remember one thing, I have come on now as a working man. Now, there is a great talk about Shakespeare. What did Shakespeare study off? If you dispute Shakespeare and look into the book, and say it is a lie, and don't tell me I am a liar (great laughter). I can tell you one thing, that Shakespeare studied – got all his studies off (A voice, 'Tripe, Bob') – no, off oyster suppers (laughter and cheers).

Mr. Blezard then, in the same strain, proceeded to recommend his audience the best drinks after oysters – whiskey or porter for those who were not teetotal, and warm milk for those who were. He condemned vinegar as the worst thing they could take to them, 'barring nooan'; administered a rebuke to the 'gallery' for the 'slack' (joking) they had given him; appealed for a fair hearing about thirty times more; offered to bet a wager that the liquor of the oyster was not 'saut watter' as was supposed by some ignorant people, but the fishes blood or jelly; recommended them, if they wanted good oysters, to buy them from him; explained how cockles ought to be cooked and 'hetten'; and finally retired from the stage in disgust, observing that he did not appear to be 'preciated'. He disappeared amid considerable hissing and laughter.

During the evening, two potatoes and an egg were thrown at the lecturer. He reappeared shortly after the conclusion of his lecture, and announced the drawing of the tickets for the barrels of oysters. He was met by a storm of hisses and uncomplimentary expressions, but he said he did not care about those things, as he made up his mind to face the devil that night. The drawing of the lots was mismanaged, and some of the audience becoming impatient, a rush was made upon the platform, and a scuffle ensued for the barrels of oysters, in the course of which the paraffin oil lamps were knocked over and broken. One of the barrels was knocked into the orchestra where the scuffle was continued. Finally, the strongest or the quickest secured the prizes, and the proceedings ended in the wildest confusion and disorder at eleven o'clock. Mr. Blezard being not a little amazed at this, his first enterprise in the lecturing line.

The 'Professor' and Mrs. Blezard regarded the evening as a triumphant success, 'especially in a business point of view'!

Following this chaotic performance, the Theatre Royal did not go 'dark' but remained in the possession of the shareholders until 1869, when William Parkinson of Scorton, Preston, a well-known operatic singer, purchased it. The theatre was then given a Regency-style façade and altered interior by Preston architect, James Hibbert, who is well known for his magnificent creation the Harris Museum and Art Gallery.

Productions were staid and the targetted clientele obvious, exemplified by one amateur dramatic performance in aid of the Blind Institute and claimed to be 'under the patronage of most of the county nobility and gentry'. The programme included 'classical' music of Verdi and Rossini, with a prologue spoken by the author, and no less than three dramatic adaptations before "God Save the Queen", and 'carriages to be ordered for half-past ten'. In 1876, financial disaster occurred, and William Parkinson sold the theatre to a local building society.

Under the lessee and management of Mr. T. Ramsey, by 1882 the theatre's exterior was further improved and considerably embellished, and the interior was rebuilt, including crimson-lined swing-bottomed chairs which replaced old leather form-seats. It was completed in order to contribute to the 1882 Preston Guild with performances of *The Black Flag*, a farcical comedy, *The Gay City*, and *Princess Trebizonde*, performed by Joseph Eldred's Opera Company. One very important visitor had arrived incognito during that Guild. The future King Edward, then Prince of Wales, attended one of the midnight performances at which Nellie Farren, Kate Vaughan and Arthur Williams played.

There was further renovation in 1898, creating a capacity of 1,700 (600 'pit', 100 stalls, 300 'boxes' and 700 gallery), and praise from the *Preston Guardian*: 'The new building is a very commodious one, including the most modern improvements as to plan of construction, whilst the decorations are superbly handsome.' Principal opera companies and leading actors of that time appeared, including Barry Sullivan and Henry Irving. The various shows staged in Edwardian Preston included *A Butterfly on the Wheel*, *Charley's Aunt*, *A Country Girl*, *East Lynne*, *The Merry Widow*, *The Only Way* (a dramatisation of *A Tale of Two Cities*), *The Quaker Girl*, *The Silver King*, *A Waltz Dream* and *The Whip* (at which a rail collison was impressively staged) plus some Shakespeare productions.

Martin Harvey starring in *The Only Way* announced from the stage that, 'the Theatre Royal was the cosiest and best theatre in the whole of the provinces'. Despite that, admission prices remained unaltered between 1904 and 1913. However, the 'writing was on the wall' for live entertainment at this illustrious venue which resisted the concept of music hall transformation. In 1911, Hugh Rain (Will Onda), the Preston impresario, began showing the latest revolution in entertainment at the time: silent films. In May 1916, Mary Pickford starred in *Esmeralda* and 'Miss Amy Sissons of the Beecham Opera Company, Covent Garden, who vocally accompanies the pictures in perfect synchronisation, will appear at each performance'.

In 1926, it was purchased by local accountant, T. H. Bailey, who was quick to react to competition created by the opening of the New Victoria cinema, and the Theatre Royal became the second town theatre to change over to full-time cinema use. In March 1927 at a showing of *Beau Geste*, the prologue was spoken by ex-Legionnaire Dunn who 'will give a graphic description of life in the foreign legion'.

The Theatre Royal, Fishergate, during the 1922 Guild celebrations. (Lancashire Library, Harris Reference Library, Preston)

The Kingsway Players, a local amateur drama group, appearing in repertory for the week commencing October 1924.

Mr. Bailey closed the theatre in 1928 for alterations, and waited until the New Victoria had a short 'run' before presenting a redesigned cinema, with double feature 'talkies', to the eager filmgoers of the town. At the opening, the *Lancashire Daily Post* reported 'Yesterday, the Theatre Royal, Preston, the most historic place of amusement in the town and, until recently, a small cosy building was re-opened after undergoing reconstruction and enlargement. A physical transformation which also made the occasion of adaptation to the new and comprehensive ideas governing up-to-date cinema houses. The auditorium has been considerably extended both upstairs and down and, together with the new foyer, waiting rooms and entrance hall, has been lavishly decorated and upholstered. The orchestra and huge Christie Unit Organ, which rise and sink at will by an ingeniously contrived lift from a sunken pit to stage level, provide music under the modern scheme, under the direction of Harry Sainsbury, a musician who has much distinguished service in Blackpool and London. The Theatre Royal has started well on its latest phase of history'.

During the era of silent films and later during World War II, music was provided by a trio comprising violin, cello and piano, featuring H. Collinson and N. Whitfield of Fulwood, Preston, and any good pianist available to provide entertainment for the audience. The Christie Unit Organ was less impressive than the one at the New Victoria, but it was nevertheless good enough to display the keyboard skills of Reginald Brown in the 1930s, followed by Bill Stokes, Frederick Schofield and Stan Taylor. It was overhauled and rebuilt in 1945, before coming to an undignified end; it was last seen on the back of a lorry, probably destined for the scrap yard.

As a cinema, the auditorium retained some of its former glory and heritage. Films could be viewed from way up on the 'top shelf of the gods' for 3d., and as a schoolboy I saw Richard Todd in *The Dam Busters* from this viewpoint. I felt like I was flying those aeroplanes in World War II! I marvelled at the well-preserved interior during the interval of the 'double bill', and began to realise that the seats were very steeply banked and that the only way to see the screen properly was to look between your knees! During the film, my experience of this unusual position was to be a constant reminder to remain calm, because I felt that any slight disturbance might result in my taking the shortest route to the stalls!

Childhood memories also came flooding back when, whilst researching this book, I came across a verse from Whittle's *History of Preston* (1837), with reference to this theatre:

> 'Tis pleasant through the loop-holes of retreat
> To peep at such a world
> To see the stir of the Great Babel
> And not to feel the crowd

The theatre finally closed its doors in December 1955 when the cinema manager, Frank Roberts, his erstwhile staff and Sooty, the theatre cat, played host to Mrs. Soman of Walton-le-Dale, Preston. Mrs. Soman was the last person to grace the famous stage as a prizewinner of a washing machine competition, and she also won and adopted Sooty, who went from large auditorium to sitting room!

June 1956 was the final curtain call for this grand Preston building, which was demolished and replaced by the ultra-modern ABC cinema. The opening was performed by Richard Todd on 14 March 1959, and the event was captured by Pathé News, who called it the most 'modern cinema of its day'. But even such a momentous beginning could not prevent the closure of the cinema after only twenty-three years, and the adjacent Theatre Street is the only reminder today of at least one hundred and eighty years of illuminating entertainment.

Ices and fruit crush will be served during the intervals at each performance

The Theatre Royal before its closure in 1955. (Lancashire Library, Harris Reference Library, Preston)

Act Two, Scene One
The Prince's Theatre, 1882–1959

Around the dawn of the 20th century, Preston's music halls came into being. Generally, they initially enjoyed economic stability, but they became increasingly overshadowed by the 1920-50s cinema boom. Despite offering a wide choice for all classes of society, it became apparent that Preston's five theatres were not going to be successful enterprises in the long term.

The town's second major theatre 'The New Gaiety Palace of Varieties', latterly the Prince's Theatre & Opera House (and finally just the Prince's Theatre) was built by Henry Hemfrey, at the corner of Crooked Lane and Tithebarn Street, in 1882. It was only a live theatre for forty years until it became the first Preston theatre to convert to full-time cinema use. In the beginning, whilst presenting operatic productions from the Carl Rosa Company, it also presented music hall to meet the growing demand from townsfolk. Indeed it was not until the Gaiety was built that there was any increase

The Prince's Theatre, Tithebarn Street. Beyond is the Regent Ballroom and the King's Palace Theatre. (Harris Museum and Art Gallery)

in the capacity of legitimate music hall. A remarkable music hall bill of 7 July 1884 contained no fewer than 454 words proclaiming the theatre, including:

> Under the sole proprietor and manager, Mr. Henry Hemfrey.
> An entirely new company this week – fresh faces and old favourites.
> Doors open 7.15pm. Overture 7.45pm.
> [Just time for a 'noggin' – things don't change!]

The varied programme featured something for everyone:

> The circus atmosphere of the Wondrous Panlos, performing acrobatically whilst on roller skates
> Little Ernest! 'The Midget Clown'
> The Levite's Combination Pantomime Troupe, a marionette show
> Miss Katie Lee, a serio-comic vocalist
> Harry Russell & Young Deutscher 'the famous Dutch Entertainers and Tyrolean Minstrels'
> The Champion Boy Tenor of the World, Percy Honri – All should hear him!
> A Novelty!

Master Percy Honri doubled up as the Young Deutscher, and was later to marry a daughter of Alderman W. H. Broadhead of the Broadhead North West Theatre Circuit, and owners of the Royal Hippodrome and King's Palace Theatres, Preston. The programme gives an insight into some of the social conditions in the late 19th century in Preston

> SPECIAL NOTICE
> Pass-out checks are not transferable.
> Seats not guaranteed.
> No money returned.
> Police in attendance and strict order enforced.
> Children must be paid for.
> Thursday: Ladies FREE night if accompanied by a Gentleman.
> Reserved seats 1/-. Sides & Promenade 6d. Pit 3d.

The Herald Printing Works, Fishergate, had provided the theatre's management with their money's worth and their literature informed the audience of what was on offer for their 'delectation and delight'. It crosses one's mind, what with the police presence and enforcement of order, whether any ladies and gentlemen would be seen in the theatre! The Gaiety was renamed the Prince's in 1889 and management invited their patrons to 'also visit the adjacent Waggon and Horses public house [now the Tithebarn] where Mr. Harry Yorke would be 'on the spot' in the harmonic room every evening'.

In 1900, the theatre almost came to a premature end whilst under the ownership of Cooper and Tullis. A farce called *A Trip to Blackpool* was playing and was destined for the Lyceum Theatre, Crewe, the following week. The events in the early hours of 28 April almost caused the manager, Robert Perrins, to have this production renamed *A*

Trip to the Knacker's Yard. At 11.20pm the previous evening, an employee had duly carried out his security checks of the theatre, only to be upstaged by an observant police officer conscientiously 'pounding his beat' in the early hours of the following morning. An imaginary police report based on the events of the night might have read like a music hall joke:

> In the early hours of Thursday 28 April 1900, I was proceeding in a westerly direction along Tithebarn Street, Preston, when my attention was drawn to the emission of smoke from the stage area of the Prince's Theatre & Opera House, which was until recently named 'The New Gaiety Palace of Varieties'. I immediately contacted my sergeant by flashing my torch. I surmised that he was still in the vicinity hereof as he had recently given me a visit.

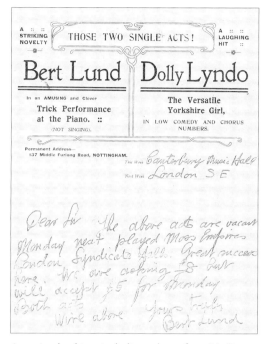

An artists booking, including a letter from Mr Bert Lund to the Theatre booking both acts mentioned for '£5 for Monday'.

> He duly instructed me to establish the source of the said smoke and call the fire brigade, as it may have been the fire-eater rehearsing his act. I discerned the emission of flames coming from the building which were definitely not from any alleged human source. I walked into the fire station and informed the station officer to take a look from the watch tower. The brigade responded immediately to the scene with six appliances and a mug of tea to steady my nerves. The **fire-eater** was later traced and denied all knowledge.

In reality, the fire station was conveniently situated opposite the Prince's, and the brigade quickly tackled the blaze, which badly damaged the stage area, dressing and property rooms. In the aftermath, the manager took 'a trip to Liverpool' for replacement sets and *A Trip to Blackpool* successfully played the Lyceum Theatre, Crewe, metaphorically bringing the house down in a rather less dramatic fashion than at the .

In August 1900, plans were before Preston Magistrates to have the damaged theatre rebuilt. The expertise of an architect, Mr. Mumford, who had dealt with three other north-west theatre fires, was sought, and he made strong safety recommendations, including the creation of a more fireproof auditorium, with additional emergency exits and improvements to corridors and staircases.

An audience capacity of 2,000 could now marvel in greater comfort and safety at the plasterwork decorating the curved balcony and extended proscenium. The renovation and improved facilities of eight new dressing rooms, 'flies' and orchestra pit, took only four months and even extended to raising the roof in time for the December opening.

After only 13 years the began to enter a state of limbo as a dedicated theatre. It was now being leased from its owner, E. H. Page, by Will Onda, who started showing films in 1913, the same year that the neighbouring King's Palace opened. In the following year there were early screenings from the battlefields of World War I, as well as live boxing. A choice of entertainment during the week commencing 25 May 1914 included Will Onda's screenings of *Neath the Lion's Paw*, a three-reel animal adventure, and four days later a 'Mammoth Boxing Entertainment with a fifteen-round contest between two of Europe's best middleweights'. In the ring were The Young Ahearn, the Dancing Master of Preston, and Harry Duncan of London. A welcome was extended to 'Ladies specially invited for a genuine night's sport'.

In the early 1920s, Will did convert the theatre into a full-time cinema, with occasional hiring for lectures, meetings and Saturday afternoon boxing matches. In those days of silent films, it was another 'laugh and scratch', with a member of staff who used a long stick to restore order to unruly children. On a more serene note, the audience did sometimes leave the theatre in an orderly fashion to the music of *Let Me Call You Sweetheart*.

Next door to the theatre was the Regent Ballroom. It is remembered by Prestonians as the place where 'true love started to blossom', just like Sam and Lizzie who met when Sam asked Lizzie to dance with her. As they twirled around in an old time waltz, Sam asked, 'Eh, Lizzie, can't we reverse?'. 'What's up, Sam,' said Lizzie, 'are you getting dizzy'. 'No,' said Sam, 'but tha's unscrewing mi wooden leg!'.

As sound films came in and World War II passed by, the cinema flourished and was managed by Arthur Cann, who had been Ivor Novello's manager, and who also managed a London theatre. It was the first town cinema to be equipped with the new 'wide screen' Cinemascope in 1953, and during that period I climbed up to the old gods of the tawdry primitive cinema to watch Humphrey Bogart in *The Caine Mutiny*. But even the blockbusters of the time were not able to stop its sad closure on 28 October 1959.

In November 1961, there was a brief final curtain-call for the when ladies from the nearby Carey Baptist Church spruced up the interior for a two-week evangelical function. Unfortunately, this didn't save the theatre from demolition in 1964 to make way for the Buckingham Bingo Hall and the St John's Shopping Arcade, in a large area of central Preston that was soon to be redeveloped. The land incorporated the old bus stations, with its Leyland Titan and single-decker Royal Tiger coaches, and the fire station with its gleaming brass-fronted Dennis red fire engines that were once the theatre's salvation. Nearby, on Church Street and opposite the Parish Church next to the former Trustee Savings Bank Head Office, was the Empire Theatre, on the site now occupied by Empire House.

The demoliton of the Theatre. (Courtesy of the *Lancashire Evening Post*)

The end of Act Two Scene One
May we now have Act Two Scene Two please?
Raise the safety curtain
Maestro, take your cue!

Act Two, Scene Two
The Empire Theatre, 1911–1974

The Empire was the last Preston theatre to be demolished, appropriately and somewhat ironically, by Albert Sparks and his team during the summer of 1976. The team moved into the Edwardian theatre in May, sixty-five years to the day since the opening of the once-majestic, 2,500-seater music hall on 22 May 1911. On that auspicious occasion, *The Lancashire Evening Post* reported that 'the inaugural performance was witnessed by a crowded house and the environs were thronged for a long while by people unable to gain admission'. That opening night featured Elsie Hulbert's Clog Dancers, a couple of comedians, Marie Schultz and Harry Tate's Company, with patrons paying four pence for gallery seats and up to ten shillings and sixpence for a four-seater box. In later times, I remember the long, narrow entrance with a big brass rail running its length, 'one side for goin' in and t'other for comin' out'. As I recall, the rules of the road applied – KEEP LEFT!

The wondrous theatre on Church Street had one of the largest and best-equipped stages in the provinces. Many Prestonians will remember the gilt-laden plasterwork of the figurines, and the boxes (for the rich 'uns), stalls, circle and gallery (the cheaper seats in the gods) whether they went to a live performance, or to see a film. It was used as a cinema from 1930 onwards and as a bingo hall from 1964 until the final

The old Preston Bus Station seems to be dwarfed by the high gable end of the Empire Theatre. (Courtesy of the *Lancashire Evening Post*)

curtain. Originally, the theatre was part of an entertainment complex opposite Preston Parish Church which included shops, a club and the Empire Hotel on Tithebarn Street, which survives to this day as a public house and was never internally connected to the theatre.

The Lancashire Daily Post said that 'the design of the theatre was in the Renaissance style of Louis XIV. There was a view of the stage from every part of the 'house'. Entrance to the stage from the street is so ample in width and height that a motorcar, fire engine or 'coach and four' could drive straight across the stage in full view of the audience'. It must have been difficult to write a plain description of the theatre. Early newspaper advertisements described the terrazzo mosaic floors, plush rose carpets, marble dados, domes, ceiling and gilded figures. Because of its many exits and elaborate fire precautions, it was said to be the 'safest building of its kind in the kingdom'.

The Empire Cinema's last 'round up' was *The Last Frontier*, starring Victor Mature. Copyright: *The Lancashire Evening Post*

The week before opening *The Lancashire Daily Post* reported,

> So unique in design, so picturesque in effect, so comfortable and commodious in every detail, and so perfectly equipped in every way is Preston's new home of entertainment that it may justly be claimed as one of the finest ever erected in the provinces, even challenging many of the most recent modern variety houses in the metropolis. 'Proud Preston' has still another just cause for pride in the possession of a theatre of varieties which has already made quite a stir in theatrical circles.
>
> The theatre entrance is obtained by the Church Street foyer, which leads to the circle and stalls. The entrance to the 'pit' and gallery, and exits from all parts of the 'house', are situated in Tithebarn Street. At the end of the entrance hall stands the box office with a corridor to the stalls on the left and the grand marble staircase leading to the main circle foyer on the right. Entering the auditorium from the circle foyer, the bold design of the proscenium immediately attracts the eye. From marble bases rise moulded pillars, to a sheer height of forty feet, meeting in a graceful arch over which two colossal sculptured figures, half-reclining, support huge electric flambeaux. In the centre of the arch, an Imperial crown surmounts an emblem of Empire. Pendant from the arch hang gracefully designed rose and gold tableau curtains, and a pair of rich

plush curtains of deep rose, draped in graceful pendant folds produce a most luxurious effect.

The proscenium is flanked by boldly-designed Georgian stage-boxes, two only on each side, the hangings and decorations being in keeping with the proscenium treatment. Each tier of boxes is crowned with an ornamental dome, and is in line with the circle and gallery. The ceiling, with its fine domed centre, hand-painted allegorical figures, and sunset-tinted panels decked with garlands of roses, crowns the general effect of luxury, spaciousness and faultless taste.

In depth, width and general design, the stage resembled that of the Theatre Royal, Manchester. It is fitted with all the latest modern improvements, the floor being an elaborate mystery of every possible shape and size of 'traps', 'cuts', 'gliders' and other devices supported on a veritable forest of struts and girders. Rooms for the orchestra, and stage hands below deck, occupy the right of the stage, and communicate with the dressing-room block behind. Everywhere the same effective type of fire appliances are met with. In the 'wings' there is a perfect maze of scenic devices and stage mechanism, stretching up to the lofty 'flies' and 'grid'. A prominent and striking feature is the costly and elaborate electrical switchboard carrying, on its polished slate-bed, switches controlling upwards of forty circuits and over two-thousand separate lights in front and behind the scenes, and the big 'arc' lamps of the frontages. From the electrician's bridge in the wings, every light and every circuit can be controlled, cut off, cut out or 'dimmed'.

The General Manager, Mr. E. P. Morgan, was manager of the Hippodrome Theatre, Manchester and then the Shepherd's Bush Empire, London [which was until recently the BBC Television Theatre]. The orchestra is intended to be one of the main attractions of the theatre, will be directed by Thomas Wrathmall, previously of the Olympia Theatre, Liverpool. The architect and Managing Director is Edwin Bush. Competent critics of theatre design, men whose wide experience gives their opinions all the weight of expert knowledge, are the first to lead the chorus of praise which will be taken up by the general public, when the new Empire opens next week.

In the arrangement of the seating in the auditorium, preserving the 'sight-lines' intact from every seat to the full width of the stage, Mr. Bush has achieved a design which betrays a touch of genius, and reflects infinite credit on himself and on the town. The spacious boldness of the auditorium plan, the graceful rake, and curve of the circle and gallery balconies, the grand arch of the proscenium, and the harmonious effect of the whole interior, lend an air of distinction which is a triumph of architectural art.

The subsidiary blocks of the scheme, the spacious shops on the Church Street frontage, the roomy and well-lit club chambers on the three upper floors, and the comfortable Empire Hotel in Tithebarn Street, are worthy adjuncts of the theatre. The hotel has two saloon bars, lounges and a commodious smoking-room on the ground floor, ample cellarage in the basement connected with every floor by a lift, a large dining-room, billiard-room, and manager's parlour on the first floor, and ample accommodation for guests on the second floor. The third floor is occupied by a well-equipped kitchen, and complete suite of service rooms and an electric goods hoist. The design, decoration and furnishing is on the same luxurious level as the theatre.

The cost of the whole scheme is £65,000. The venture is bold and praiseworthy, the proprietors having faith in the good taste of the people of Preston, to crown their enterprise with the hallmark of appreciation. Shakespeare wrote, 'Tis not in mortals to command success. But we'll do more, Sempronius: we'll deserve it,' which fitly describes this great scheme. With the ever-popular variety performances, the management also intends to stage musical comedy, pantomime and grand opera at suitable periods. A determined effort is to be made to exclude rigidly from all performances that bugbear of the variety stage, doubtful humour, and to present at all times clean, wholesome amusement, of the highest quality obtainable.

Edwin Bush, the Managing Director, had promised twice-nightly variety, musical comedy, pantomime and grand opera. Like a sign of things to come, a bioscope presentation called *The Haunted House* was seen on the opening night and, in August 1911, a week of films was shown. During the glory days of the theatre up to 1918, musicals, pantomimes, plays, professional grand opera and amateur operatic productions also featured. Leading music hall artists of the day, like comedian, Robb Wilton, appeared frequently.

There were one or two comedians off stage too. A friend, local historian Nellie Carbis, once told me a funny story about queuing for food during World War I. When one saw a queue forming it was second nature to join it. One old woman had joined a theatre queue and tapped the arm of the woman in front of her. 'Would yer mind telling me, luv, what we are queuing for?' '*The Tales of Hoffmann*', was the reply. 'Oh well,' said the old woman, 'Ah might as well 'av one, it'll do fer't cat!'

Printed programmes not only illustrate the range of productions which have been presented in Preston over the years; they also give an insight into the commercial life of the town. In the 1920s, gramophones and wax records could be obtained from H. S. Mosley, 64 Friargate; you could phone Lofthouse on Preston 1279, a char-à-banc proprietor of 415 New Hall Lane; Greenwood, Guildhall Street, provided music, pianos and the latest song-sheets; and Thomas Mears, Fishergate, exhibited a full page of their merchandise.

On Monday 15 November 1920, the programme boasted a return visit from the famous Allington Charnley Grand Opera Company, the largest touring opera company in the world, with over one hundred artists and full orchestra. They presented a different opera each night including Verdi's *Il Trovatore* on Tuesday, Bizet's *Carmen* on Wednesday, Gounod's *Faust* on Thursday matinee, Verdi's *Un Ballo in Maschera* (The Masked Ball) on Thursday evening, and Wagner's *Tannhäuser* on Friday. If all this was too much, Loxham's Garages advertised fifteen different models of Morris motorcars at prices from £162 with full twelve months' insurance included!

EMPIRE THEATRE, PRESTON
Commencing MONDAY, August 30th, 1926
ONCE NIGHTLY at 7-30   MATINEE : THURSDAY at 2-15

Cecil Barth
and
Hayden Coffin
produce the Light Opera

Lionel and
Clarissa

· by arrangement with Nigel Playfair ·

direct from the Lyric Opera House, London

☆ All Star Cast ☆

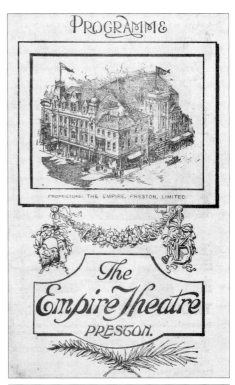

PROGRAMME

PROPRIETORS: THE EMPIRE, PRESTON, LIMITED.

The
Empire Theatre
PRESTON.

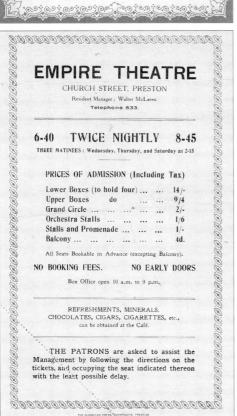

EMPIRE THEATRE

CHURCH STREET, PRESTON

Resident Manager : Walter McLaren.

Telephone 533.

6-40   TWICE NIGHTLY   8-45

THREE MATINEES : Wednesday, Thursday, and Saturday at 2-15

PRICES OF ADMISSION (Including Tax)

Lower Boxes (to hold four)	14/-
Upper Boxes do	9/4
Grand Circle	2/-
Orchestra Stalls	1/6
Stalls and Promenade	1/-
Balcony	4d.

All Seats Bookable in Advance (excepting Balcony).

NO BOOKING FEES.   NO EARLY DOORS

Box Office open 10 a.m. to 9 p.m.

REFRESHMENTS, MINERALS,
CHOCOLATES, CIGARS, CIGARETTES, etc.,
can be obtained at the Café.

THE PATRONS are asked to assist the
Management by following the directions on the
tickets, and occupying the seat indicated thereon
with the least possible delay.

THE GUARDIAN PRESS, FISHERGATE, PRESTON

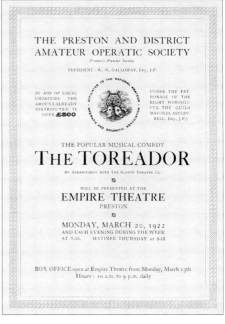

THE PRESTON AND DISTRICT
AMATEUR OPERATIC SOCIETY

Preston's Premier Society

PRESIDENT : W. W. GALLOWAY, Esq., J.P.

IN AID OF LOCAL
CHARITIES.   THE
AMOUNT ALREADY
DISTRIBUTED IS
OVER **£800**

UNDER THE PAT-
RONAGE OF THE
RIGHT WORSHIP-
FUL THE GUILD
MAYOR (H. ASTLEY-
BELL, Esq., J.P.)

THE POPULAR MUSICAL COMEDY

THE TOREADOR

By Arrangement with The Gaiety Theatre Co.

WILL BE PRESENTED AT THE

EMPIRE THEATRE
PRESTON

MONDAY, MARCH 20, 1922
AND EACH EVENING DURING THE WEEK
AT 7-15.   MATINEE THURSDAY AT 8-15

BOX OFFICE open at Empire Theatre from Monday, March 13th
Hours : 10 a.m. to 9 p.m. daily

A selection of Empire Theatre programmes
from the 1920s, and the reverse of a 1930
programme, showing the 'Twice Nightly'
admission charges.

The Preston & District Amateur Operatic Society and the Preston Light Opera Company both presented delightful productions and lavishly illustrated programmes of their productions. The Operatic Society's first production was a concert at the Theatre Royal on 1 May 1912, in aid of the *Titanic* Relief Fund. On the fateful day of the disaster itself, the Empire was presenting Hetty King, billed on 15 April 1912 as the first visit to Preston of the world famous male impersonator.

When the clouds of World War I had lifted, the Operatic Society presented the following annual productions at the Empire from 1919-25: *Gipsy Love*, *Miss Hook of Holland*, *The Mikado*, *The Toreador*, *A Country Girl*, *The Belle of New York* and *San Toy*. The Light Opera Company's repertoire included *The Quaker Girl* (1920), *Floradora* (1922), *Lilac Domino* (1925), *A Waltz Dream* (1926). In 1926, the renowned Ivor Novello emerged from the stage door in Tithebarn Street, dressed in a black cloak, white silk scarf, white gloves and top hat, having appeared in a play called *The Rat*. George Robey and Marie Blanche were in *Bits and Pieces* during the week commencing 31 January 1927. In 1928, a revue inappropriately called *Come Again* starring Jose Collins almost ended live performances at the theatre when it lost £400 in a week. But in October that year, the Light Opera Company's production of *Sally* was a good 'curtain-raiser' for their annual dance held at the Bull & Royal Hotel on 7 November 1928. Tickets for this sumptuous occasion were seven shillings and sixpence, including supper.

George Formby Jnr headed a twice-nightly comedy revue *Formby Night Out* for the week commencing 15 April 1929. During the summer of 1930, Frank Cariello's Repertory Company staged the last live performances with a season of plays, billed as 'your last chance to see your favourite stars before the Empire goes over to talkies'. That year, Edwin Bush sold it to Federated Estates and Walter McClaren remained as manager of the new cinema. It was obvious that many patrons had fond memories of its past and the final live performance was reported, as below, in *The Lancashire Daily Post* on 4 August 1930:

The Last Curtain

With the singing of *Auld Lang Syne*, the stage and audience linked over the footlights by the holding of hands, 'legitimate' stagecraft took its farewell curtain at the Empire Theatre on Saturday evening. It was a simple and touching little ceremony which moved some of the more emotional of the big audience to tears, and left few present unaffected by the general regret which changes of this kind evoke.

Preston certainly bade farewell to the Empire as a theatre in worthy manner. Long before the first of the bi-nightly performances had concluded, there were long queues lined up at the pay-boxes, and the foyers and stairways were thronged with those who had booked their seats. For the last show there was not an empty seat. The circle held its full quota, the promenade was packed, the stalls and 'pit' were full, each 'box' was occupied, and through the rails of the gallery the occupants poked their faces, determined not to miss a single incident, however trifling, in what they regarded as 'the very last show'.

The march of science

When the play ended, Frank G. Cariello and his repertory company, who concluded an eight weeks' engagement at the theatre with a presentation of *A Butterfly on the Wheel*, had to withstand a bombardment of gifts and flowers. Mr. Cariello followed with an admirable little speech. If there were any who had expected a denouncement of the 'talkies' usurping that which had been designed for other purposes, they were disappointed. Mr. Cariello returned thanks for the many kindnesses Preston had extended to him, during his stay in the town. "Complete financial success has not attended our venture, it is true," he said, "but after all, great painters have died in garrets and we as artists do not always look solely upon the mercenary side of things to indicate our successes. We have been happy here, and if I get an opportunity to bring my colleagues before you again, I shall seize upon it very eagerly."

Leaving the personal side, he spoke about the changeover. He had been intimately associated with the transformation of two of Preston's leading theatres, the Theatre Royal and now the Empire. Did they expect him to say he was sorry about the change? he asked. Personally he did not think that was an occasion for sympathy. It was just the luck of the game, and after all the world could not withstand the march of time, and science and mechanics.

Personal associations retained

Continuing, he said that any concern that would take over a building, and maintain it for the purposes of providing entertainment and employing people, deserved all the support that could be given. He made an eloquent appeal for the new venture, and when a voice from the gallery made an expression of disagreement with the sentiment, Mr. Cariello looking upwards said very quietly, "That it is not the true voice of the 'gods'". Saying 'Au Revoir', the speaker paid a warm tribute to Walter McClaren, the manager of the theatre, who he declared had been most charming and delightful to himself and his company. Mr. McClaren had watched every production through, had given his opinions upon them and offered much helpful advice. The services of Mr. McClaren as manager have been retained by the new company, and some of the staff have been re-engaged, so that on the personal side the old associations are largely preserved.

The theatre is closed this week, to enable an ambitious decorative scheme which includes alterations and reupholstering of the seats to be carried out. One of Lon Chaney's greatest pictures, 'The Phantom of the Opera', now attracting huge crowds in London, and three other 'star' productions will be featured at the re-opening fixed for Monday 11 August. The Western Electric Supreme Sound System claimed to be the perfection of mechanical phonetics has been installed, and paying due regard to the industrial conditions prices have been made very modest. The Empire is the fourth Preston theatre to transfer its allegiance from the 'legitimate' stage to cinema. The first was the Prince's, then the King's Palace, [transitional] followed by the Theatre Royal and on Saturday, the Empire.

The Phantom of the Opera was apparently a 'serious risk to health', as the management advised patrons that 'Red Cross nurses are in attendance' and 'those with a nervous disposition are advised to attend the afternoon performances so you will not be afraid to go home in the dark!'. During World War II, the gods were closed off for safety reasons and the reduced capacity was to be permanent at 1,066. Imaginative advertising propaganda continued through the years, and was similar to the days of the old music hall, with slogans such as 'the house built for sound and perfect talkies at last'. In the 1950s it was the first cinema to have a Cinemascope screen, which filled the whole of the proscenium and was dubbed 'on our mammoth wonder screen'. The first film shown on the big screen was *The Robe*.

In 1963, Preston Musical Comedy Society had no permanent base for productions, and persuaded the management to remove the 'wonder screen' for

FABULOUS GALA OPENING WEEK ATTRACTIONS INCLUDE . . .

OPENING NIGHT - THURSDAY, 13th AUG.

PERSONAL APPEARANCE OF

ELSIE TANNER

PAT PHOENIX of T.V.'s "CORONATION STREET"

GUARANTEED PRIZE MONEY DURING THE EVENING AT LEAST **£300**

LUCKY FOR SOME

Any member winning on No. 13 will receive DOUBLE PRIZE MONEY

Friday, 14th Aug.	Saturday, 15th Aug.	Sunday, 16th Aug.
Big Prize Money on all the Bingo Games Plus . . . THE FABULOUS STAR 1/- QUICKIE WITH A GUARANTEED PAYOUT OF AT LEAST **£100** Dozens of Free Weekend Joints	A SUPER-DE-LUXE **REFRIGERATOR** MUST BE WON TONIGHT ON A FREE GAME Plus Huge Prize Money on all the usual Big Bingo Games	**LUCKY LEGS NIGHT** 200 PAIRS OF NYLONS **FREE** and Big Prize Money on all normal games

MONDAY, 17th AUGUST

GROCERIES GALORE

FREE! FREE! FREE!
AND BIG PRIZE MONEY FOR ALL WINNERS!

Tuesday, 18th August	Wednesday, 19th August
DARBY & JOAN NIGHT Fabulous First Week Offer **Surprise Gift For All** Plus Double Prize Money on normal games on production of Pension Book	**GOOD CHEER NIGHT** LOTS OF BOTTLES Free! Free! and Big Cash Prizes on all Bingo Games

AT EVERY AFTERNOON SESSION – A FREE 18-PIECE TEA SET TO ALL FULL HOUSE WINNERS!

The Student Prince turned out to be the penultimate stage performance in May 1964. On August 13 of the same year Pat Phoenix (Elsie Tanner from *Coronation Street*) hastened the departure of the nomadic Preston Musical Comedy Society when she graced the stage to announce the gala opening of the Empire Star Bingo Club.

seven days for their production of *The Lilac Domino*. Remarkably, the stage machinery, dressing rooms and other items that had lain dormant for over thirty years were brought back to life, and sounds from the orchestra pit once again reverberated throughout the theatre. The Empire was re-born but for all too short a period.

My most poignant memory of the theatre was witnessing a further re-awakening in 1964 when the PMCS staged *The Student Prince*, and a truly memorable and nostalgic experience was shared with my old grandma, who remembered the shows of days long ago. Alas, this production was the last for the society at this venue. The 'silver screen' had to make way for bingo when the Leeds-based Star Group bought it in 1964. The final film, the aptly-titled *The Last Frontier*, spooled through the projector, with this 'last picture show' starring Victor Mature, who symbolically signalled the demise of the great Hollywood legends of the 1930s to 1950s. A final stage performance, on 13

August that year by Pat Phoenix (Elsie Tanner of ITV's *Coronation Street*) launched the last few years of its life as a bingo hall. The Empire closed when the Star Group transferred its bingo club to the former Ritz cinema across the road in 1974.

The doors were opened again only to admit Albert Sparks, and his team of workers, to the darkened and derelict theatre two years later. If the spirits of yesteryear's artists had been looking down upon them, it would have been a formidable and awesome line-up of stars, witnessed by a standing ovation from ordinary people experiencing an unforgettable period of true heart-warming entertainment. A time for contemplation during the next intermission, hopefully not interrupted by the sounds of pneumatic drills and falling masonry.

Are you interested in becoming a permanent booked seat patron for all twice-nightly performances at the theatre? If so, select your night, select your favourite seat, give your name & address to the box office & your seat will be reserved for you each week! Full details are available at the box office.

A rare photograph of the Light Opera Company's 1928 production of *Sally* at The Empire. (Courtesy of Peter Vickers)

Reprise

The last of Preston's original theatres was demolished in 1976. The Empire's demise represented the end of an era. Unlike the Public Hall, no one mounted a tenacious, well-orchestrated campaign to revive any of Preston's theatres and save them from demolition. The Guild Hall complex had metaphorically risen from the ashes of former theatres strewn across the town centre, and the financial viability of any additional venue would have been in serious doubt. Many blows had struck live entertainment broadside throughout the region during the '50s and this pattern continued unabated, both in Preston and in neighbouring towns.

About this time, John Osborne wrote 'the music hall is dying and with it a significant part of England. Some of the heart of England has gone; something that belonged to everyone, for this is truly a folk art'. In 1959, Sir Laurence Olivier epitomised this dying era when he played the part of a struggling and broken down music hall comic in John Osborne's film *The Entertainer*, shot on location in Morecambe. The seedy Alhambra Theatre on West End promenade was a perfect choice for the film company. Olivier himself probably felt less at home in the old Alhambra than Archie Rice, the character he portrayed, however! The film also featured interior shots of the Winter Gardens (formerly Victoria Pavilion) which had its exterior restored with the help of a grant from The National Lottery. Unfortunately, it is improbable that it will ever become a full-time theatre again and some compromise seems more likely.

Manchester's Opera House and Palace Theatre both went dark in the 1970s. Ken Dodd was instrumental in saving the Palace and also took the initiative to try to save Liverpool's Royal Court Theatre for theatrical productions. The Royal Court has since been used essentially as a rock venue. Manchester's Opera House had degenerated, like Blackpool's Grand Theatre, to 'eyes down and look in' before being rescued from the national wave of bingo-mania and oblivion. The two Manchester theatres now prosper commercially and, together with the restoration of the Royal Exchange Theatre, serve the whole of the North West.

At Blackpool, the Department of the Environment saved the beautiful Grand Theatre from demolition in the nick of time during the 1970s, when it was given listed building status. Full credit should be given to the individuals who formed the Friends of the Grand, and fought a long and hard battle to save this outstanding example of the work of Victorian theatre architect, Frank Matcham. The building is now one of Blackpool's treasures.

The founder of the Friends of the Grand was venerable campaigner Major A. Burt-Briggs of Lytham St Annes, a grandson of William Henry Broadhead, of the Lancashire-based theatre and show business entrepreneur Broadhead family. Many people acknowledge Major Burt-Briggs' leadership qualities that helped save The Grand for future generations. I am also especially grateful to him for information concerning the Broadhead family and their theatres, which included Preston's King's Palace and Royal Hippodrome. As a lead into Act Three, when the spotlight is placed firmly on the history of these two venues, there now follows a short history of this remarkable family.

Mjor A. Burt-Briggs, T.D., founder of the Friends of the Grand.

Ovation – The Broadhead Family

About a hundred years ago, this famed entrepreneurial family built up an empire throughout the Red Rose County, which eventually encompassed sixteen theatres and a dance hall. The circuit was known to acrobats, comics, glamorous dancing girls, magicians, singers and a plethora of music hall entertainers as the 'bread and butter' tour, because regular bookings did not produce the high wages of the Moss Empire and other prestigious theatre owners.

Broadhead's talent scout, Ernest Simms, had the job of watching artists' performances and, if they were found to be suitable for the Broadhead 'circuit', were booked with a wage that was guaranteed while they toured their huge Baroque-designed music halls. The artists developed their acts by judging the level of enthusiasm from audiences to the new 'gags' in case they ever played the notorious Glasgow Empire Theatre, where they knew they would have to suffer an onslaught of tomatoes and other fruit if the gags didn't go down well!

It was vital that all theatres had the maximum number of 'bums on seats', as well as those standing in permitted areas, in order to create a full house atmosphere, as well as making a profit!

William Henry Broadhead and his sons played a major role in the establishment of music hall in the North West. William Henry was born in Smethwick, Stafford-shire, in 1848, and his job as a builder took him all over the country. After meeting and marrying Mary Ann Birch in Manchester, he founded his own building firm with a head office in Tib Street, just off Piccadilly, in Manchester.

In 1883, he moved to a 'famous seaside town called Blackpool, noted for fresh air and fun'. Three years later, he took over the Prince of Wales Baths next to the Prince of Wales Theatre, which was managed by Thomas Sergenson, who opened the Grand Theatre in 1894. This was the

William Henry Broadhead.

Members of the Broadhead family with their theatre managers, about 1921. Percy Baynham (Sonny) Broadhead (in short trousers) became the last manager of the King's Palace Theatre, Preston. His father, Percy Baynham Broadhead (Senior), is on his left making a presentation.

Alderman W. H. Broadhead and his son William Birch Broadhead outside Kensington House, his residence on South Promenade, Blackpool, near the New Yorker Café at the corner of Alexander Road and South Promenade, c. 1905/6

same year that another famous building, Blackpool Tower, was opened. The Baths staged variety shows as well as pioneering swimming and aqua displays, the latter acts inspiring the finale of the circus shows at the adjacent Tower for many years. The Baths site eventually became the Palace Variety Theatre, Cinema and Ballroom, but sadly all were demolished. A Lewis's department store was then built on that site, which now occupies the Mecca disco and Woolworth's store.

Throughout their long business career, Broadhead's business policy to anticipate and react to change was very much a hallmark of the management of theatres. A few years later, William Henry became a Liberal Alderman and Director of Blackpool Tower and South Pier companies. In November 1905, he was elected Mayor and served a second term of office in 1910-11. The family was quick to exploit the need for music hall theatres for the working classes and, as an impresario, William's motto for entertainment was 'Quick, Clean, Smart and Bright'.

William Henry had four daughters and two sons, William (Willie) Birch Broadhead and Percy Baynham Broadhead. It was Willie who suggested adopting Blackpool's motto of 'Progress', still used to this day, whilst attending his father's Mayoral banquet in 1905. His speech included the statement 'That if the fathers and mothers of Lancashire would adopt Blackpool's motto of 'Progress', they would never fear for the prosperity of Blackpool'.

Willie had already displayed foresight and vision for the future of the business. Previously he had produced many of the aqua shows, as well as appearing in them as a comedian and a stuntman. The business really began when he first managed to persuade his father to invest his capital in a theatre in Manchester. He earmarked sites for his theatres and, in 1895, the first built was the Osborne in Oldham Road, Manchester, followed by thirteen in Ashton-under-Lyne, Bury, Eccles, Liverpool, Manchester, Preston and Salford. In 1909, he opened the Palais-de-Danse at Ashton-under-Lyne, and the same year acquired the Winter Gardens, Morecambe. Three years later, he purchased the Lyceum Theatre, Eccles which was later renamed the Crown (see appendix for a full list). Annie, a daughter of William Henry, married the well-known music hall performer, Percy Honri, who once said that 'W. H. Broadhead and Sons were builders of theatres rather than bidders for theatres someone else had built'.

Influenced by Frank Matcham, who designed the Grand Theatre, Blackpool, Willie designed most of the theatres, and the person responsible for interpreting his ideas was Mr. J. J. Allen, who was an architect employed by W. H. Broadhead & Sons. The building and contracting department was based in Thomas Street, Manchester, and erected most of the theatres quite quickly.

After the Boer War, theatres were getting back into profit, and the most successful of these were in the Broadhead circuit. In Preston, Willie built the Royal Hippodrome in 1905, in less than eight months without modern construction equipment. The magnificence of the auditorium will be considered later, but facilities backstage were less practical, as the height of the 'flies' was restricted by the theatre's reduced gable end, and there was a lack of space for painting and building scenery.

I well remember laughing at the comic ad-libbing during a pantomime when a scenery backdrop became stuck and half suspended across the proscenium. This unscripted interlude was one of the highlights of the show, notwithstanding the stage manager's sigh of relief, when the panto dames' red and yellow cottage eventually made a safe stage landing. Frugal and skimpy conditions backstage may have been based on the Broadhead philosophy that, in case of poor box office 'returns', all theatres could be re-designed for use as factories. Neither of the Preston theatres had to resort to this, although other uses were contemplated. An early programme promised 'dramatic productions of an uplifting moral nature for the working classes at prices they can afford'. The company's ideals included being advocates of temperance, with no provision made for the consumption of alcohol, and the Hippodrome was without a licensed bar until 1934.

W.H. Broadhead & Sons knew how to make money and William Henry ('The Management') toured his theatres in a Daimler limousine. At his home on the promenade in Blackpool, the 'returns' of all his theatres were sent for scrutiny, and were usually opened with a special paper knife by one of his grandchildren. However, this cosy business routine was tragically interrupted in 1907. His son Willie was returning home to Manchester by car from London and, after stopping to help a stranded motorist, he caught a severe cold that turned to pneumonia and sadly died in February of that year, at the age of 34. Over three hundred mourners attended the funeral, with a large band from all the family theatres playing Chopin's Funeral March at the head of the cortège.

Willie's loss to the company was very great. An assistant to his father, he was considered to be the architect, contractor, furnisher and decorator for most of the theatres. He always maintained that the respectable citizen could take his wife and children to any of their productions, find them free from vulgarity, and at a price well within his means. Alert and cheerful, he would often 'drop in' at any one of the performances at some point in the evening.

An anonymous artist writing in *The Performer* 1931, commented that he was once persuaded to accept a five-week engagement on the Broadhead circuit at £1 less than his normal fee. At the conclusion of the first 'house', a gentleman came to his dressing room and said 'I have come to apologise for cutting you down in your salary. One of our managers had reported that you were not worth the price quoted by your agent. Having seen your act tonight, I consider that you are worth more, so here is £5 to make up the difference. I will give you the remainder of the tour on your terms'. That man was William Birch Broadhead – a fair and kindly man indeed.

The second son, Percy Baynham, also had a son, Percy Baynham Broadhead Junior, and both managed the theatres in the same efficient way. When William Henry sought a licence for the last of his theatres, the King's Palace, in 1913 it was claimed to be an embarrassing addition to the town's theatrical provision. At the hearing, the owners of the Empire, and Theatre Royal jointly argued that not one of Preston's theatres realised a decent return on capital invested in them. The owner of the stated that 'my 'house' has suffered with the opening of the Empire and the Royal Hippodrome should be closed to compensate for the opening of the King's Palace'.

William Henry refused to disclose the Royal Hippodrome's profitability, arguing that the theatres and cinemas were crowded on Mondays and Saturdays and sometimes on Thursdays. He got his licence for the huge 2,600-seat venue, with room for another 400 standing, after convincingly stating that 'the prosperity of Preston for live entertainment was greater than in other towns and the Lancashire people really do enjoy themselves'. He also revealed he had been interested in buying the Empire.

Many requests were made for use of all the Broadhead theatres during World War I and they were always granted and, in most cases, no charges were made. When the public's taste began to change to films, it became obvious that the theatrical investment had not been justified after all. The King's Palace was converted for cinema use as early as 1917, together with the slogan 'Come what time you like, stay as long as you like'. This was an early innovation for continuous film performances, and in the '20s the venue was dubbed 'The King's Palace of Music and Pictures'.

Not long after it switched back to music hall, William Henry resisted a quarter of a million pound offer from a film distributor wanting to purchase the whole chain of theatres as cinema outlets. His son, Percy Baynham Snr, persuaded him that he was the only man in the country personally to own seventeen theatres, and he should retain them. 'Broadhead's magnificent halls for the delectation of the people' would be around for a little longer.

Sadly their creator would not. Alderman W. H. Broadhead died in 1931, at the age of 83 years. His legacy of 'taking amusement and entertainment to the people at prices to reach the multitude' was now left to his son, Percy Baynham Snr, who took over as manager. After closely watching the changing fortunes of their two Preston theatres, he sold the Royal Hippodrome just prior to the outbreak of World War II. Percy Baynham (Sonny) Broadhead Jnr. was to be appointed sole manager of the King's Palace until its closure in 1955.

In the late '50s, the advent of television sounded the death knell for theatres, and over the next twenty years about half of the Broadhead circuit was demolished. The remaining eight have been converted to clubs, television studios and other uses. Mecca bought the Hulme Hippodrome, and Liverpool Pavilion survives as a bingo hall, but none have so far retained or returned to their original use. The King's Palace and Royal Hippodrome in Preston have long since made way for town centre redevelopment sites and their artists, managers and staff are now but a memory.

Indeed, Percy Baynham Broadhead Snr died at the height of the closures in 1955. His son, formerly residing in Fulwood, Preston, died in retirement at Ross-on-Wye in 1964. Gone, but not entirely forgotten, the history of the Broadheads and their theatres is very much a part of the social, cultural and show business history of north-west England.

Friargate and the Royal Hippodrome, 1905. The decorative iron canopy nestling between the old
Hoop & Crown pub, and the ironmongers and woodworking machinists of R. Slinger & Son, was at
the entrance to a walk-through arcade leading to the theatre and Black Horse Yard, adjacent to which
is the Black Horse pub which is still situated at the corner of Orchard Street. (Courtesy of the
Lancashire Evening Post)

*Remember – 'Dramatic productions of an uplifting moral nature for the
working classes at prices they can afford' Make it 'Quick, clean, smart and
bright'.*
WHB (The Management)

Act Three, Scene One
The Royal Hippodrome, 1905–1957

King Edward VII was on the throne, the Boer War was over, two World Wars had yet to be fought and a liner named *Titanic* was to sink in the North Atlantic Ocean with tremendous loss of life. On Friargate electric tramcars had almost replaced horse-drawn carriages, new motorised carriage-cars chugged up the brow and merchandise was delivered to shop traders by horse-drawn carts and steam traction engines. Close by, impressive steam trains thundered by under a plume of white smoke whilst departing from the railway station.

The trams and carriages stopped close to the Royal Hippodrome to discharge the ladies and gentlemen, elegantly dressed for an evening's entertainment, who queued beneath the entrance canopy and gradually traversed the long covered walkway to the theatre's crimson entrance doors. After payment at the box office, a kindly attendant directed the 'toffs' to the 'boxes' and the remainder to the stalls and grand circle, where they awaited in anticipatory eagerness to bestow their patronage on an inspired performance, in the splendid surroundings of a brand new theatre.

It was the Broadheads who conceived the need to further increase entertainment for the townsfolk, as well as to increase their theatre empire in Preston. Plans were submitted to the Corporation on 4 May 1904, and building commenced almost immediately on Friargate, adjacent to Black Horse Yard, and was completed after only eight months. In the preceding ten years there had been at least seven theatrical fires in Lancashire including one at the Theatre, Preston. The Royal Hippodrome was to be lit by gas and electricity, which meant that fire inspections had to be rigorous.

The theatre exits had been well studied and it was claimed that a 'full house' could be emptied in three minutes. All 2,500 seats commanded a full view of the stage and there was a spacious waiting room for the benefit of the second 'house' patrons of the evening, where daily newspapers and magazines were provided. The interior decor was designed by Mr Leighton, an artist who had acquired considerable notoriety for his work when he was a pupil of Herr Komier. The first manager was Mr Freeman who had come from another Broadhead theatre – the Queens Park Hippodrome, Manchester – and was very experienced. He was proud of the motto of the Broadheads: 'Quick, Clean, Smart and Bright'.

A local historian of the time reported further in *The Lancashire Daily Post*:

> Time and again has a thoroughly up to date music hall and variety theatre been promised for Preston but it was not until some eight or nine months ago that definite arrangements for the construction of such a building was

brought to the notice of the public. Messrs W. H. Broadhead & Sons, the well-known theatre proprietors, took the initiative and have purchased land in and behind Friargate. A large quantity of old property has been demolished and on the site has arisen a most substantial and pretty Hippodrome, which is certainly a decided acquisition to the list of Preston's places of amusement. The building, which is one of the largest of its kind in the country, is approached from Friargate by means of an arcade passage, having shops on either side, and the façade of this is terra cotta and when completed will stand out as one of the architectural features of the locality. Other entrances are by way of Black Horse Yard and at the main entrance is a handsome vestibule, decorated with white and gold, with coloured leaded lights.

So far as the interior is concerned, there is abundant evidence that no expense has been spared. The ceiling is divided into eight oblong panels with splendid Egyptian mountings in fibrous plaster. and these are bordered by friezes representing garlands of flowers. The proscenium is in Ionic style with Renaissance panels and friezes and on each side are statues representing 'Repose' and 'Silence', supported by brackets, imitative of the heads of Satyrs. Messrs. J. Alberti & Sons, Manchester and Italy have executed the fibrous plasterwork. The stage, which is an exceptionally large and lofty one, is fitted with a fireproof safety curtain, and the lighting is arranged so that there is little danger of fire. On each side is a handsomely furnished private box, prettily decorated. All the main walls are furnished with rich crimson art paper which harmonises extremely well with the gold and white used in all other decorations.

As regards accommodation, special attention has been paid to the comfort of patrons. The seating is well arranged and is of luxurious character. For sixpence one may secure a cosy folding seat in the stalls and the circle is fitted with all the latest appliances. It is estimated that the seating capacity will be slightly over 2000. Prices are box seats, two shillings; circle, one shilling; stalls, sixpence; and pit, three-pence. In the matter of fire appliances, the Hippodrome is well supplied with everything on the latest principle, including patent sprinklers.

The scheme of lighting is a novel one and is carried out both by means of gas and electricity. A gas engine with a 250 horse power capacity has been installed and this is used for driving the dynamos and no less than 1800 electric bulbs are used. So far as ventilation and sanitary matters are concerned they have received careful attention in the hands of experts. Absolute detached lavatories for ladies and gentlemen throughout the theatre.

The main structure has been planned and built by Messrs. Broadhead & Sons while much of the lighting and decoration has been carried out by members of their staff. Every compliment is to be paid to the proprietors for having brought the undertaking to a successful conclusion. Sub-contractors for the enterprise are as follows: fire appliances, Rose & Co.,Salford; seating, Messrs. Hargreaves, Orchard Street, Preston; carpets and linoleum, Butler & Hadfield, 5 Friargate, Preston; tableau curtains, orchestra rail and draperies, A. R. Dean

& Son, Birmingham; steel and ironwork, Foster Bros., Hope Foundry, Preston; moulding and timber, Page Taylor, Preston; and joinery work, Walker & Cottam, Preston.

A final inspection of the premises took place on Saturday 14 January 1905 when Mr W. P. Park, Chairman of the Inspection Committee, complimented Mr Broadhead on his enterprise and, after Mr Broadhead agreed to some minor changes, a licence was granted. That night the theatre was thrown open to the general public for a preview and, between 7.30pm and 10.00pm, many thousands of Prestonians surged through the entrance, passing compliments that it certainly filled a long-felt gap in the town's entertainment provision.

The following Monday in Edwardian Preston brought blizzards, and gangs of men with salt tried to stop tramline points from freezing up. This did not prevent the formal opening at the Monday matinee with a 'full house' and 'standing room only'. At 2.30pm the orchestra played the National Anthem, the fireproof safety curtain was raised and, as the stage was revealed, hearty rounds of cheers resounded through the theatre.

A special variety programme had been arranged. Charles Coburn, looking well after his tour of the USA, was warmly welcomed with his quaint songs and sketches including renditions of 'Coster's Friendly League', 'The Man who broke the Bank at Monte Carlo' and 'Two Lovely Black Eyes', were fully appreciated.

Probably the most talented animal performer in the country presented Chard's Dogs. There were also amazing cycling feats from the Seven Proveanies, the Barbusians clever acrobats, the Four Maisands in their eccentric musical performance, as well as clever harmonising from the Louisianan Serenaders, and Davis & Davis, Marie Winsome, and Winnie Scott – all splendid 'turns'.

The programme passed off without a hitch and the management was congratulated on their success. Notwithstanding the inclement weather, there were good houses at both performances in the evening. From the first performance, the Broadhead traditions had to be strictly followed. Staff had to be 'shiningly' clean and immaculately dressed and live up to the catchphrase 'On the ball', uttered by the Manager of the theatre, Walter Hume. Before opening, he paraded all the staff who dealt with the public and inspected their hands, nails and general appearance. He maintained that the box office and programme sellers' hands, faces and hairstyle must be up to the standards expected by patrons at that time. Today, such an inspection would have caused Walter innumerable problems and delayed the proceedings. I imagine that the ear, eyebrow and nose rings and tattoos piercing of today would have been a bigger attraction than the artistes!

Daring escapologist Houdini never forgot his visit to the theatre in 1906. He promoted his act by first visiting Preston Prison on Stanley Street to uphold his reputation that no lock, straitjacket or prison could ever hold him. He almost lost the challenge after finding the prison had unusual cell locks and handcuffs, and it took him three hours to set himself free. He injured his hand in making his escape and recorded his thanks to the young doctor who treated him. He said afterwards, 'Preston should be equally proud of its prison as its North End football team. Your prison is one of the most secure places I have ever come across'. Later he wrote in his diary 'that Preston is one of the best places I have visited', even though he almost lost his international reputation here. Whilst not reported at the time, rumour had it that once in the cell he wasn't making much progress until one of the guards told him what was on the tea menu. This message seemed to introduce the necessary urgency because, within the hour, he was walking out of the prison!

The Royal Hippodrome occasionally used Will Onda's bioscope to blend early silent films with music hall acts, whilst apparently having a laugh at the expense of the clergy. In February 1907, it was showing animated pictures, including *The Curate's Dilemma*, and eleven months later, *The Curate and His Double*. Even before theatre censorship, satire was evident and no one escaped the net. The use of primitive film projection equipment was part of the evolution of music hall. At the Royal Hippodrome, the phase was soon transcended, even though special equipment had been installed to show the visit to the town of King George V and Queen Mary in 1913.

Marie Lloyd was one of the last classic music hall acts, who so epitomised the era, appearing in the Hippodrome, Preston, in 1911. Typically, she would have engendered a tremendous rapport and intimacy between artist and audience, with her comic routines and songs including 'Oh, Mr. Porter' and 'My Old Man (said follow the band and don't dilly-dally on the way)'. Imagine having a seat in the front stalls on that night!

No old theatre can be without a story of a theatre ghost, and in January 1913, Alman Correge and his partner, John Smith, were presenting their comedy juggling act. John's part of the routine was to throw himself all over the stage, and trip over all the props. Towards the end of the act, it was his custom to lie down at the side of the stage and pretend he was asleep. On that night, he commenced a very long sleep indeed and, when the curtain was raised for them to take a bow, he didn't spring to his feet. The audience thought it was all part of the act, but he was carried off and the resident Police Constable William Hamer, who always sat at the back of the stalls to check that no offensive actions or words were portrayed, was called to the stage door to administer first aid.

Sadly, poor John was already dead, and the subsequent inquest verdict recorded natural causes. True to theatrical tradition the show carried on, and so does John Smith! Forty-six years later, the theatre was demolished. A department store was built on the site, and the manager's office is situated at about the spot where John lay down and died. He always smoked cigars and people often comment on the unusual smell in the office, especially as smoking is not permitted in any part of the store today. The many music hall legends and other performers, including Harry Champion, Gracie Fields, Florrie Ford, Marie Lloyd, George Formby and Little Tich have long been immortalised in different ways.

The programme pictured on the opposite page shows the typical admission prices in the early days of the Hippodrome, at a time when the young men of the town would be ordered to 'pack up their troubles in their old kit bag' and sent to war a few weeks afterwards. Many would never return to their beloved proud town, to 'keep the home fires burning'. In 1916, Florrie Ford no doubt had her sights set on the 'Long Way to Tipperary'.

Old theatre programmes speak volumes and the nature of music hall is characterised by cheap admission prices, the topography of the theatre, and the advertisements they contain reflect the social and trading conditions of the time. One such carries an advertisement for R. Bennett, Lune Street, who claimed they were 'paying best prices and prompt cash for false teeth'. Ugh!! If there were to be any complaints at the theatre – for example, 'the ladies not removing their hats' – then patrons could 'communicate with Percy Baynham Broadhead Snr. at his Hippodrome office in Manchester, or have a word with the theatre's General Manager, Mr. H. Winstanley, after the show'.

In the 'roaring twenties', the theatre became a focus of the 'world of variety' with revues, musicals, opera, pantomime and circus, which even in the street included the spectacle of a procession of elephants proceeding to the stage door in Black Horse Yard! 'Our Gracie' Fields graced the stage in November 1922 and there was a Charleston Dance Competition in May 1927.

During the following decade, the Broadheads promoted their pantomimes and endeavoured to have nine of them touring their theatres each Christmas with yet another slogan: 'Pantomimes, arranged constructed for laughter purposes only. That is, to entertain and amuse, to cheer you up in these unsettled times'. It was perhaps a sign of the times during the economic Depression that out of an original fifty pantomime titles, only twenty were running by 1935. In that year *Goody Two Shoes* drew record crowds to the show, produced by the forty-strong company led by Teddy White, during its two week run. Even though times were hard, most families managed to afford to pay and see the Christmas 'panto'.

The theatre was also having to compete with the first 'talkies' being shown at Preston's cinemas, including the New Victoria, which had opened its doors in September 1928. Slogans appeared stating that the Royal Hippodrome provided 'living artists not talking pictures'. In 1934, a continuous live programme was presented from 10am to 10pm to meet the challenge of all-day

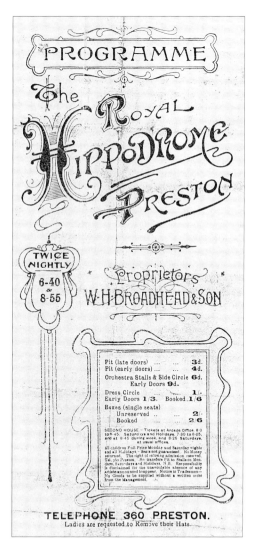

Royal Hippodrome Theatre 20 July 1914 programme.

cinema shows. Those programmes became mildly erotic by the standards of the day, and Percy Broadhead commented 'that standards were not always living up to the ideals first established by the Broadheads'. Risqué young ladies billed as 'Lady Godiva' or 'the inimitable breathing marble', a young Australian lady posing only in enamel-type paint, did nothing to address the problem of dwindling audiences to cinemas, and may indeed have exacerbated it.

In July 1939 *Love on the Dole* played for a second time, after a 1935 performance starring Robert Morley. The production turned out to be a financial disaster and led to the theatre staff themselves being on the dole. The Broadheads also bowed out from ownership shortly before the outbreak of World War II, and the theatre remained 'dark' until it was re-opened by a new owner, Claude Talbot, on 5 May 1941 with a production called *The Secrets of the BBC*. On the first night, in the company of the Mayor and the Mayoress, the new management pledged to carry on 'in the same old tradition of the best in variety and musical comedy and in the same atmosphere of comfort and cheeriness that made the old Hippodrome so popular'.

Admission prices were cheap at 1/- to 2/6, and the long-term outlook now seemed to be rosy once more. Claude Talbot brought an imaginative approach to the changing needs of theatre. Traditional variety acts, musicals, opera and more plays helped to

No No Nanette. An October 1941 post-London production unusually featured photographs of the cast. 'I want to be happy, but we won't be happy, 'til we've made you happy too', were cheery lyrics in a heart-warming production in troubled times.

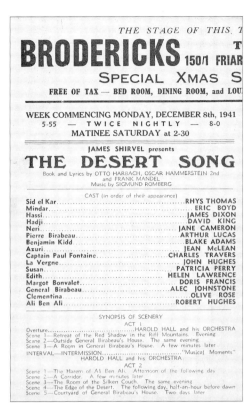

THE STAGE OF THIS. T

BRODERICKS 150/1 FRIAR

SPECIAL XMAS S

FREE OF TAX — BED ROOM, DINING ROOM, and LOU

WEEK COMMENCING MONDAY, DECEMBER 8th, 1941
5-55 — TWICE NIGHTLY — 8-0
MATINEE SATURDAY at 2-30

JAMES SHIRVEL presents

THE DESERT SONG

Book and Lyrics by OTTO HARBACH, OSCAR HAMMERSTEIN 2nd
and FRANK MANDEL
Music by SIGMUND ROMBERG

CAST (in order of their appearance)

Sid el Kar	RHYS THOMAS
Mindar	ERIC BOYD
Hassi	JAMES DIXON
Hadji	DAVID KING
Neri	JANE CAMERON
Pierre Birabeau	ARTHUR LUCAS
Benjamin Kidd	BLAKE ADAMS
Azuri	JEAN McLEAN
Captain Paul Fontaine	CHARLES TRAVERS
La Vergne	JOHN HUGHES
Susan	PATRICIA PERRY
Edith	HELEN LAWRENCE
Margot Bonvalet	DORIS FRANCIS
General Birabeau	ALEC JOHNSTONE
Clementina	OLIVE ROSE
Ali Ben Ali	ROBERT HUGHES

SYNOPSIS OF SCENERY

ACT 1

Overture.................................HAROLD HALL and his ORCHESTRA
Scene 1—Retreat of the Red Shadow in the Riff Mountains. Evening
Scene 2—Outside General Birabeau's House. The same evening
Scene 3—A Room in General Birabeau's House. A few minutes later
INTERVAL—INTERMISSION.........................."Musical Moments"
HAROLD HALL and his ORCHESTRA

ACT 2

Scene 1—The Harem of Ali Ben Ali. Afternoon of the following day
Scene 2—A Corridor. A few minutes later
Scene 3—The Room of the Silken Couch. The same evening
Scene 4—The Edge of the Desert. The following day, half-an-hour before dawn
Scene 5—Courtyard of General Birabeau's House. Two days later

The Desert Song. This December 1941 production was an inspiration for six-year-old Roy Barraclough, who was in the audience, and subsequently embarked on his famous stage and television career. One wonders if another youngster, comedian John Inman, born at his father's hairdresser's shop on Fishergate Hill, got similar inspiration for his future employment.

Richard Tauber. Richard Tauber and Charles Hawtrey appeared on 25 January 1943. The famous tenor had also appeared here on 1 September 1941 in Lehar's operetta *The Land of Smiles*, and Charles went on to become a television and film star, remembered for his appearances in ITV's *The Army Game* and as a regular in the *Carry On* films.
(Courtesy of the *Lancashire Evening Post*)

slow the general demise of music hall. Representative programmes of the period 1941-7 certainly illustrate Claude's policy of high-class productions and theatrical diversity.

The next production was by the noted Shakespeare company, the London-based Old Vic Theatre, in a new play *Shirley*. On 18 May 1942, the Old Vic presented *The Merchant of Venice.*

As well as Shakespeare plays other cultural performances included grand and light opera. The D'Oyle Carte Opera company played at least four times during 1942-4 with their Gilbert & Sullivan productions. *The Yeomen of the Guard* was performed on 27 February 1943, and was followed a week later by the famous French play *Damaged Goods.* George Bernard Shaw considered the play to be 'a public danger that needs a public warning'. It was restricted to adults only but was no doubt very innocuous by today's standards.

The National Philharmonic Orchestra played for a week commencing 17 May 1943,

Tel. 357311 COMMERCIAL CATERING A SPECIALITY
ARTHUR STOCK
OLD DOG HOTEL, CHURCH STREET, PRESTON.
Lion Ales at their best

CLOTHES for Men and Boys
MOORE'S
137 FRIARGATE PRESTON

T. C. RAINFORD & SONS
95 FISHERGATE
and Branches

Butchers
Provision Merchants,
Restauranteurs,
at
3, ORCHARD St.,
PRESTON.

Ask for
SEED'S
When you ask for
Mineral Waters
Obtainable in This Theatre.

WEEK COMMENCING MONDAY, MAY 17th, 1943
Once Nightly at 7-0.   Matinees Thursday and Saturday at 2-30
HAROLD FIELDING presents
INTERNATIONAL MUSIC
with the
NATIONAL PHILHARMONIC ORCHESTRA
AND WORLD FAMOUS SOLOISTS

Mon., May 17 at 7-0
BEETHOVEN FOURTH SYMPHONY
EINE KLEINE NACHTMUSIK (Mozart) etc.
Soloist:
EILEEN JOYCE
in the
GRIEG PIANO CONCERTO
WARSAW CONCERTO
Conductor: **JULIAN CLIFFORD**

Tues., May 18 at 7-0
BEETHOVEN FIFTH SYMPHONY
SIEGFRIED IDYLL (Wagner) etc.
SOLOMON
in the
SCHUMANN PIANO CONCERTO
Conductor: **JULIAN CLIFFORD**

Wed., May 19 at 7-0
NEW WORLD SYMPHONY (Dvorak)
OBERON OVERTURE (Weber) etc.
LOUIS KENTNER
in the
EMPEROR CONCERTO (Beethoven)
Conductor: **RUDOLPH DUNBAR**

Thurs., May 20 at 2-30 and 7-0
(Same Programme and Soloists at each performance)
EGMONT OVERTURE (Beethoven),
RUY BLAS OVERTURE (Mendelssohn) etc.
ALBERT SAMMONS
in the
BEETHOVEN VIOLIN CONCERTO
and
WEINGARTEN
in the
LISZT E FLAT PIANO CONCERTO
Conductor: **WILLIAM REES**

Fri., May 21 at 7-0
TSCHAIKOWSKY PROGRAMME including
FIFTH SYMPHONY and NUTCRACKER SUITE etc.
MARK HAMBOURG
in the
B FLAT MINOR PIANO CONCERTO
Conductor: **JAN HURST**

Sat., May 22 at 2-30
BEETHOVEN SEVENTH SYMPHONY etc.
IDA HAENDEL
in the
TSCHAIKOWSKY VIOLIN CONCERTO
MICHAL HAMBOURG
in the
CHOPIN F MINOR PIANO CONCERTO
Conductor: **JAN HURST**

Sat., May 22 at 7-0
SCHUBERT UNFINISHED SYMPHONY,
MASTERSINGERS OVERTURE (Wagner) etc.
MARK HAMBOURG
in the
HUNGARIAN FANTASY FOR PIANO and ORCHESTRA
(Liszt)
AND A GROUP OF PIANO SOLI
Conductor: **JAN HURST**

BRADSHAW'S Motor House Ltd.
MARSH LANE
PRESTON
Can now supply the following Vehicles against M.O.W.T. permit
FORDSON
10cwt. Van
FORDSON
4/6 Ton Tipper
FORDSON
4/6 Ton L.W.B.Truck

A BEER IN A THOUSAND FOR THE MILLION
LION ALES
EVERY DROP TIP-TOP !
BEST IN 1830
—STILL THE BEST
OBTAINABLE IN THE BARS OF THIS THEATRE   LION BREWERY, BLACKBURN

A programme for the National Philharmonic Orchestra when they performed in Preston in 1943. The programme advertisements are typical of the period.

and what a line-up of famous soloists there were, including the Russian pianist Mark Hambourg on two evenings. Albert Sammons played the Beethoven Violin Concerto which he had first played at a London hotel in 1908, when Sir Thomas Beecham heard him and, judging him excellent in virtuosity and musicianship, engaged him as leader of his orchestra.

Solomon (actually Solomon Cutner) was an English pianist who made his first public appearance at the Queen's Hall, London at the age of eight playing Tchaikovsky's First Piano Concerto. I can only say I wish I had been there – all week! I will have to cherish my memory of the Royal Liverpool Philharmonic Orchestra performing one afternoon to a whole Hippodrome theatre full of fellow school children – my first experience of the RLPO and a big orchestra.

On 4 June 1945, Jack Hylton brought a play set in an 18th-century Orkney Island castle called *Duet for Two Hands* by Mary Hayley Bell. The cast included Elwyn Brook Jones and the playwright's husband, a young John Mills. Mrs. D. M. Scholes of Fulwood was in the audience and managed to get her programme signed by John and Elwyn during the interval. The original programme is shown bearing the actor's signatures and I am especially grateful to Mrs. Scholes for her contribution. At the time of writing, Sir John Mills is in his 90th year. Long before *Great Expectations*, Scott

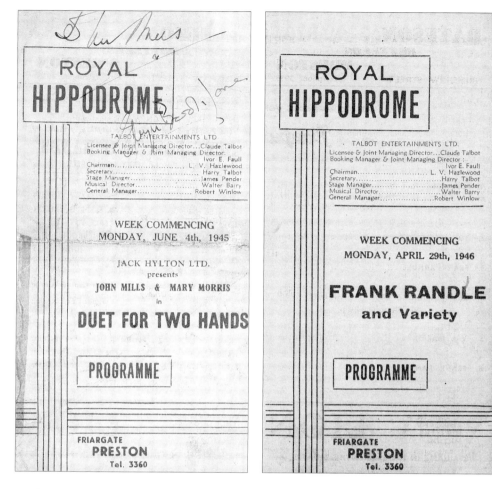

Another great Lancashire comedian, Frank ('we supped sum stuff toneet') Randle, sang his little ditty "I'm happy when I'm hiking" and then uttered his 'Get off me foot!' catchphrase. He played in Randle's Scandals in 1945 and the programme above right featured him in a variety show that began on 29 April 1946. The programme on the left has autographs from John Mills (top) and Elwyn Brook-Jones, both of whom appeared in *Duet for Two Hands* in 1945.

of the Antarctic, Ryan's Daughter (for which he received an Oscar, and a whole host of memorable films, musicals and plays, plain John was just a jobbing actor. Leslie Cant, a scenic designer and artist and former member of the Salberg Players has commented that during the war it was not unusual for London-based productions to tour the provinces.

Variety acts predominated during and after World War II. Hilarious Hylda Baker in conversation with her famous 'man dressed up as a woman' stooge Cynthia, 'Be soon, I said, be soon!'. There was the dry humour of Jimmy Jewel (of Jewel & (Ben) Warriss fame), and amusing anecdotes from Gert and Daisy Warner, sisters of actor Jack. Also on offer was ventriloquist Peter Brough and 'Archie Andrews'; crooner Cavan

O'Connor; 'Britain's brightest entertainers', the two Leslie's – Sarony & Holmes; Comedian and violinist, Sandy Powell ('Can you hear me, mother?'); American singer and ukelele player 'Two Ton' Tessie O'Shea; Billy Cotton and his Band; and Lancashire comedian, Albert Modley, who appeared in the Christmas 1945 pantomime *Jack and the Beanstalk*.

The theatre went out to a much wider audience on three occasions in 1947 when Northern Music Hall was broadcast via wireless radio. This 'shot in the arm' was much-needed at the time, following several indifferent revues without the calibre of artists such as John Mills.

The Salberg Players

The theatre got a major boost and change of direction on 14 July 1947 when Reginald Salberg presented a season of plays scheduled to last a few weeks. The first play was *The Hasty Heart*. In the booklet produced for the opening shows Salberg reflected that 'The directors of the Royal Hippodrome and ourselves feel that there is a need in

PEGGY MOUNT

SHE was with a concert party all through the war; her high spot during this time was the night before D-Day going from one temporary camp to another every hour to entertain the soldiers before they went off.

She has toured nearly all over England, but it is the Yorkshire moors she loves the best. She is passionately fond of Haworth, the Bronte country, and always likes to go back whenever she is near enough.

She is very fond of swimming and riding ; she reads detective fiction and her favourite actor is Sir Laurence Olivier.

A special booklet was produced by Reginald Salberg giving details of the company and four opening plays in 1949.

The cast of a 29 November 1948 production of Salberg's *Love in a Mist* featured prominently on the cover of the programme, and included a young Leslie Cant (middle row), whose recollections appear later in this book.

Preston for a theatre which will concern itself for a large part of the year with good plays, well presented. We will hope to fill that need. We hope your decision will be favourable, because on it rests the length of our stay at this theatre with which I feel in love at first sight'. It must have been a favourable public reaction because, after the initial run, Salberg stayed for eight years!

In 1949 Reginald Salberg presented a pictorial souvenir of the repertory players. 'It's hard to visualise Preston without the Salberg Players now', remarked a patron. The affinity was so strong that the weekly plays became a permanent part of the town's culture, and the Salberg Players changed their name to the Preston Repertory Company. It was often described as the best weekly 'rep.' company in Northern England. I have spoken to many former patrons of the Royal Hippodrome and there is no doubt that Salberg is a name that is sentimentally cherished. Patrons looked forward to a good selection of plays, acted with aplomb by the regular actors, and they queued 'once nightly' in the covered passage to hand over their hard-earned money at the box office in return for an evening's entertainment. Once again the theatre was playing to well-supported houses.

The company players were well established in their profession, and several went on to become famous stars of London's West End, and television and cinema screens. A young Peggy Mount, for example, appeared in *Sailor Beware*. During World War II, Peggy had been with a concert party and the night before D-Day she took her important role in the comedy from one temporary camp to another, entertaining the armed forces before they embarked to foreign lands.

Other members of the company are still well-known today: Doreen Andrew, John Barron, Derek Benfield, Jean Burgess, John Dearth, Frederick Jaeger, Nancy Mansfield and Charles Mardel, showed great versatility in farce, thrillers and melodrama.

Productions were of such a high standard that they gave actors a good springboard to fame on stage and screen, with vaulable experience being gained through the pressure of producing a different show each week! Husband and wife acting teams started their real off-stage romances, whilst existing couples in the company included John Barron and Joan Peart, Derek Benfield and Susan Lyall-Grant, John Dearth and Kate Lindsay, Kenneth Keeling and Doreen Andrew, and David Rose and Valerie Andrews. It seemed infinitely better than 'romantic late suppers' at frugal theatrical digs!

The list of plays presented appear endless and some of the most successful at the box office were *The Merchant of Venice, Rebecca, A Streetcar named Desire*, and heart-throb John Dearth in *Death of a Salesman*. John became a big name in London's West End and on television, along with Frederick Jaeger, Nancy Mansfield and Peggy Mount. Charles Mardel became a Canadian Broadcasting Corporation announcer. Bradford-born actor and playwright Derek Benfield had television success with *Hetty Wainthrop Investigates* with Patricia Routledge. A big film star of the time, Jean Kent, made a guest appearance in a Robert MacDougall play *Escapade* on 6 September 1954, which was the company's 340th play and drew one of the theatre's biggest audiences for months.

An up-and-coming young actor called Leonard Rossiter appeared in *The Gay Dog*

"The Gay Dog"
By JOSEPH COLTON

Characters in order of appearance :

Maggie	ANNE GOADBY
Sally	EILEEN MAYERS
Mrs. James	PEARL CATLIN
Spud Ryan	PETER WYATT
Peggy Gowland	DOROTHEA McCLOSKEY
Jim Gay	HAROLD MAJOR
Bill Gay	ALAN FOSS
Minnie Gay	FIONA DORNING
Bert Gay	LEONARD ROSSITER
Peter	ROBERT STEPHENS
Leslie Gowland	MICHAEL HARRISON
Rev. Mr. Gowland	ANTHONY FINIGAN

On 13 September 1954, Leonard Rossiter took the part of Bert Gay in *The Gay Dog* in the Preston Repertory Company's 341st production. In the 1950s, Lennie starred in several productions by Preston Repertory Company, including their last offering of *Love in a Mist* in 1955. (Photograph of Leonard Rossiter courtesy of the *Lancashire Evening Post*)

at the Hippodrome, and of course later became famous as Rigsby in the TV series *Rising Damp*. In the 1970s, I had occasion to speak to him outside the Guild Hall where he was in a play at the Charter Theatre, and he affectionately informed me, 'I started off here you know, at the Hippodrome down the road'. I went to see him in that play, Charles Dickens' *A Christmas Carol*, and he gave a virtuoso performance as Scrooge. I felt so sad when this hard-working actor died so prematurely and I will always remember my brief encounter with him.

Inevitably television became increasingly popular after the BBC's live coverage of the Queen's Coronation in 1953 and the introduction of ITV, and the Preston Repertory Company began to lose its regular patrons. When it ended its extended stay in March 1955, it was another nail in the coffin for the ailing theatre's fortunes. In reality, Preston could no longer support two large commercial theatres. The King's Palace closed on 19 February 1955, and its dedicated orchestra transferred to the Royal Hippodrome. In just over two years time, the band would again be looking for work.

A grand variety show marked the theatre's 50th anniversary in July 1955, and the orchestra played for a young Welsh-born singer, Shirley Bassey, who gained international recognition as a superstar, but failed to restore the declining audience. Shirley returned to Preston twenty years later to take the Guild Hall by storm with a packed house and numerous encores.

A young 'Scouse git', and Tony Blair's future father-in-law, Anthony Booth, featured in *A Girl called Sadie* on 2 April 1956. In May 1957, a group called the Hippodrome Players closed the theatre down forever with a play called *The Tender Trap*. The programme produced for this pre-closure show had a blank last page where the following week's fayre would normally have been fanfared. As so often happens on these sad occasions, people came back for one last nostalgic Saturday night visit, and it was their biggest audience in years. The manager, Claude Talbot, had a poignant message for them: 'The date 25 May 1957 should be remembered with shame by every citizen of this town who claims to enjoy the theatre. I don't think there will ever be a live theatre in Preston again.' With the Charter Theatre opening sixteen years later and the continued use of the Playhouse Theatre by numerous amateur groups, this prediction didn't turn out to be true. However, it was the last of Preston's commercial theatres, one that had a professional rep. company, and the final link with music hall. In other words, the end of an era.

The theatre stood empty for two more years, after which it was demolished and replaced by a C & A department store. It died with some dignity, never having suffered the ignominy of conversion to a full-time cinema or bingo hall throughout its 52-year history. Only the ghost of juggler John Smith reputedly provides a

By 1953, the writing was one the wall for the Hippodrome as well as for *Cinderella*.

Friargate, 9 July 1959. This picture features period milk churns against the façade of the derelict Hippodrome. (Harris Museum and Art Gallery, Preston)

link with its glorious past – and needless to say, I would love to meet him and offer him a cigar!

It's the final curtain as the theatre is demolished in August 1959. (Courtesy of the *Lancashire Evening Post*)

There will now be a short intermission. Tea and coffee will be served during each interval in the circle lounge and in the theatre

Act Three, Scene Two: King's Palace Theatre, 1913–1955

In the 16th and 17th centuries, the original site of this theatre was a garden that belonged to the Parish Church old vicarage, formerly situated on the town centre side of Bishopgate. Many years later, the site was occupied by a Broadhead-acquired roller-skating rink bounded by Old Vicarage Lane, Bishopgate and Tithebarn Street. The skating rink was known as The Empress and William Henry Broadhead's daughter, Hilda, was a member. Sir Cuthbert de Hoghton also enjoyed the facilities and apparently excelled as a skater.

William Henry decided to build the last of his theatres here, and the skaters became the sacrificial lambs when plans were passed by Preston Corporation in September 1912. Building started at once and was completed in January 1913, at a time when the Broadhead name was well established in the town following the opening in 1905 of

A rare photograph of the interior of the King's Palace Theatre. (Harris Museum and Art Gallery, Preston)

the Royal Hippodrome. But there was to be a controversial police court hearing when a licence was applied for his latest creation.

The theatre was different from other Broadhead projects according to newspaper reports of the time. Most of his other theatres had been built on a square basis, but this one had a glazed terracotta exterior and was clean and very smart from the outside. It also marked a change in design internally and in the auditorium there was a three-domed ceiling, with a proscenium arch supported by colonnades of *rouge-et-noir* marble. The decorations had been carried out by Mr Bartlett, who had been responsible for interior work at the Stoll Theatre, London. Like the Empire, Preston, the style of the decorations was Louis XIV in an attractive colour scheme of cream and gold, painted with illustrations of allegorical subjects, in which the Muses were represented together with allied goddesses cast in high relief.

All the curtains and drapes were of apple-green shade and produced a pleasant effect, and the carpets were of *rose-de-barri* pink. The fauteuil stall seats were of new and rich crimson plush, and in the pit there was room for 1350 patrons with very ample legroom. Everything personified grace and beauty, and had been created with elegance and refinement.

I can remember the large gaping boxes either side of the proscenium, and the cavernous nature of the auditorium, with a single-tier circle. It must have been one of the largest theatres in the country before the new Opera House in Blackpool opened in the 1930s. The stage was 75-feet wide with a depth of 35 feet, and was large enough to accommodate any type of travelling production. The electrical switchboard, manufactured in Preston, controlled over 1,000 points that could be operated by one person.

On Monday 3 February 1913 at Preston Borough Police Court, William Henry sought a public licence to operate under the Theatres Act for a Music, Singing and Dancing Licence under the Preston Improvement Act. The theatre was up to date and compared well with the best in Manchester and Liverpool, and was in a central position bounded by roads on three sides.

Following an on-site visit, the reconvened court listened to evidence for and against the application. The grounds for refusal were that 'another theatre was not required, it was badly sited, the public did not wish another theatre, and the value of existing theatres in the town would be depreciated if another licence was granted'. It was pointed out that the only real objection was the last point, but it was not a matter for the magistrates to take into consideration at all. Together with his barrister, William Henry argued his case. The assistant clerk stated that 'the application and plans had been correctly submitted and that this session had been specially called under the Theatres Act'.

William Henry, making application, stated that 'I am the owner of theatres in and around Lancashire and herewith show plans that the new King's Palace will accommodate 3,000 people comfortably – 24 in 'boxes', 485 in the stalls, 570 in the pit stalls, 810 in the pit, and 670 in the circle. These figures together with the standing accommodation will cope with a 3,000-strong audience. There are fourteen exit doors, and all doors and walls between the stage and auditorium are armoured and fireproof.

The whole building is fitted with water sprinklers and all passages and staircases are concrete. The building met all the requirements of the London County Council and it is estimated that it can be cleared, in an orderly way, of all persons in three minutes'. There was no provision for 'bioscope entertainment', or intoxicating liquor, although there were two large lounges providing light refreshments.

Evidence of the seating capacity of the Empire, Prince's Theatre, Royal Hippodrome and Theatre Royal were produced showing that, together with the twelve cinemas in the town, there was accommodation for 100,000 patrons a week. Another objector pointed out that Blackburn, with a population of 133,000, against Preston's 117,000, only had four theatres and seven cinemas. When William Henry was asked why he had built the King's Palace, he replied 'I am thinking of making a profit!'. When it was suggested to him that perhaps Preston was not a progressive town, he replied, 'Perhaps it wants waking up a bit!', at which there was much laughter. Asked if he had bought the Empire would he have built the King's Palace, he replied, 'I can't answer that question as the site was doing very well as a skating rink at that time'.

Many other statements were made against the granting of a licence, and all from the opposition theatre owners in Preston. They said they would withdraw objections if William Henry were to surrender the licence for the Royal Hippodrome. The members of the Police Court bench withdrew and, after an absence of fifteen minutes to consider their decision, the Chairman announced that the Justices had, by a substantial majority, agreed to the granting of a licence until 28 May, the annual licensing day.

This may have overturned the equilibrium of the four other theatres but there are many people with fond memories of this huge music hall theatre offering comic routines, dance, drama, pantomime and song, all playing to full houses on Friday and Saturday nights. On opening it was described by the Broadhead propaganda machine as 'another Messrs. Broadhead & Sons achievement in the raising of magnificent halls for the delectation of the people and the most up-to-date theatre in Lancashire'.

The first theatre manager was William J. Boyle, better known as Johnny Boyle, the orchestra was under the direction of Robert Peel, and Edward Leigh became the scenic artist. Harry Winstanley, who had given unstinting loyalty to the Broadhead family since 1883, had now become General Manager of the circuit. The circuit was anxious to keep up the big following for variety, both here and at the Royal Hippodrome, on which the family's traditions were firmly anchored. It was to be 'the most dramatic theatre in Lancashire bringing opera productions from the Grand Junction, Manchester and pantomimes from the Pavilion, Liverpool', all integral parts of the Broadhead 'bread and butter' circuit.

During opening week, comedian Jack Pleasants was topping the bill at the Empire, the Prince's had already succumbed to showing films, the Royal Hippodrome was presenting a family pantomime, and the George Alexander Company was presenting *Bella Donna* at the Theatre Royal.

The opening night at the King's Palace was on Thursday 6 February 1913 and, before the first act, the orchestra delivered a spirited playing of the National Anthem which drew a standing ovation from the large audience. Top of the bill were Charles Barnold's

Dog & Monkey Actors in a one-act comedy pantomime *A Hot Time in Dogville*, featuring Dan, the Drunken Dog.

A local newspaper critic of the day reported:

> this is a realistic comedy that might have been made up out of Aesop's or La Fontaine's fables. The dogs and monkeys perform human actions and exhibit human foibles in a grave and earnest manner that only heightens the caricature of 'the lords of creation'. They do everything but speak. Indeed speech or bark is not necessary. The silent pantomime is more expressive and all the time no trainer is to be seen.
>
> The curtain rises on a New York street scene with a cafe, saloon, sausage shop and a few houses. A droll comedy is enacted in which dogs and monkeys tricked out [dressed up] as bar tenders, butchers, nursemaids, police officers, scavengers and soldiers appear, and gravely go through a screaming travesty without a yelp or a bark. The most finished comedian of the lot, the 'canine Dan Leno' so-to-speak, is a dog who has dined 'not wisely, but too well', and passes through various stages of intoxication, till he collapses helplessly in the roadway. A monkey police officer is furtively watching him from round the corner, and when he has reached the stage of apparent incapability, he takes him into custody. Finding the task a difficult one, he rings up the police station, and presently a van appears into which the incapable diner-out is ignominiously dragged and driven off triumphantly to the lock-up.

There were other ludicrous episodes, including an elopement, which all excited wonder and applause. The rest of the 'turns' were all enthusiastically reported, including the John Tiller Twelve Sunshine Girls, just back from a successful tour of the USA. Four months later, and more in keeping with the Broadhead propaganda, there was a series of plays of an 'uplifting moral nature', featuring the Frank Adams Dramatic Repertoire Company. An interesting play called *The Royal Divorce* had been touring the world for twenty-five years and was the story of Napoleon and Josephine featuring the real-life great-grandson of Napoleon, Monsieur Juan Bonaparte, and Violet Ellicott as his wife. Every Friday night was a Grand Souvenir Night, and on this occasion every lady in the audience was presented with a magnificent rolled-gold pendant, containing portraits of the Emperor and Josephine. The appropriate overture for this play, Eckersley's descriptive and realistic 'The Battle of Waterloo', was played by the Band of the Third Batallion of the East Lancashire Regiment under the direction of Band-master, Mr W. Godley.

Archie Pitt, destined to become Gracie Field's first husband, played the Broadhead tour in 1915 with *Yes, I Think So* and, following the opening at the Hulme Hippodrome, Manchester, the second port of call was Preston. Many more wonderful nights of entertainment were organised in the next year or two for the dedicated patrons. There were suggestions that the theatre had been constructed allowing for easy alteration to factory use should there have been poor box office returns, which was consistent with

Broadhead's built-in security against loss, but none of the Preston theatres had to suffer this indignity. However, it was converted to cinema use as early as 1917.

Saturation point had already been reached in terms of the number of theatres open vis-à-vis the size of the local population. This multiplicity of live entertainment meant that the managers of the Prince's and Theatre Royal had also been quick to adapt to the exploitation of the new silent movies, and now this theatre was doing the same. In the 1920s, William Henry reversed the trend, announcing that because there were too many cinemas in Preston it would return to its original use. So seven years after becoming a cinema, the silver screen was removed and the safety curtain reinstated.

Comedian and violinist Ted Ray made his first UK stage appearance here in 1927 and, in keeping with the Broadhead's policy of giving artists 'opportunity knocks', ballad singer Donald Peers 'filled-in' one week which was his first time on the professional stage. Donald was such a success that he was engaged to return a few weeks later, and was top of the bill.

During the late 1920s, Ernest Simms, the Broadhead field scout, was quick to recognise the talent of a young music hall artist called George Formby Junior. Eric wrote in his diary, 'I feel sure this comedian will rapidly make good'. Wigan-born George made a big name for himself and, at one time, was the UK's highest-paid star of stage and screen, making twenty films between 1934 and 1947. He was famous for his risqué songs, accompanied by his ukelele, and everyone knew what he meant with his 'Little Stick of Blackpool Rock', 'Auntie Maggie's Remedy', and what he observed 'When I'm Cleaning Windows'.

George topped the bill at the theatre several times and, on one occasion, left the stage and performed his act in the stalls and then in the circle, amidst his delighted audience. He was also a regular artist at the Empire. In his later years he lived in Preston, and could be seen driving around, displaying his toothy grin, and no doubt uttering his catchphrase 'Turned out nice again' followed by a chuckle! Sadly, in March 1961, at the age of only 56, he died of heart failure at St Joseph's Hospital, Preston.

As in all theatres, there are lots of tales to tell. At the King's Palace, during the performance by the Great Levant, his last illusion was the 'Lady in the Trunk'. The 'Lady' was placed in the 'Trunk' and, after numerous stabbings of the trunk with spear and swords, the 'Trunk' would be opened and found to be empty. The 'Lady' would then appear from the rear of the theatre to take her bow, and also find some time to change costume as well. However, on this occasion she lost her way, and couldn't find the correct door to make her entrance. She had to return by the stage door that took some time to open, and then appeared on stage looking extremely wet and sorry for herself. In the unscripted waiting period the Great Levant had to resort to a considerable amount of ad libbing, which was quite out of character.

Another tale, from 1930, involves Koringa & Friends, where a very beautiful, scantily-clad lady (Koringa) performed with her snakes and alligators. The first part of the act involved placing an alligator on two plinths, accompanied by appropriate music and gestures and, by some 'miracle', the reptile would become very stiff and she would climb on top of it. On this occasion, the alligator took offence at the humiliation, turned its head and bit Koringa's thigh, and both disappeared into the orchestra pit. Normally members of an orchestra take their time moving out of their domain, but on receiving this unusual 'encore' they made a rapid exit! Meanwhile, Koringa dragged the reptile by its tail, up the side steps alongside the stage box, to screams from its occupants, onto the stage and into the wings. She was able to give the usual performance at the second house that evening, in a typical example of the well-known theatre addage 'the show must go on'.

During World War II, the old music hall theatre really sprang back to life, engendering confidence and optimism during traumatic times. The Nazi threat of bombing was bravely ignored by patrons in theatres throughout the country, which provided an escape from the problems of the world at that time. Printed programmes did, however, include certain warnings:

> Please bring your gas mask with you!
> A.R.P. NOTICE
> Should there be an Air Raid Warning, the Manager would announce the same
> from the stage so that patrons could leave the building if desired,
> or stay and see the show all through, as the artists,
> orchestra and staff will carry on as usual
> after the warning has been given.
> Reduced prices for members of H. M. Forces.

The atmosphere of wartime theatre in Preston is encapsulated by the programmes of the time which were always basic in their format and gave details of Broadhead's

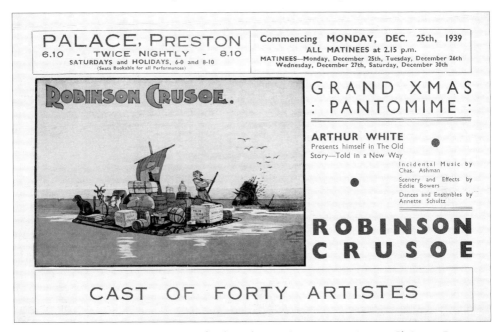

A one-off, lavishly illustrated programme for the Robinson Crusoe pantomime on Christmas Day 1939.

Singer and comedienne Tessie O'Shea. 'Two Ton' Tessie from the USA was a 'regular' on the 'bread-and-butter' circuit. This battered programme from 1941 shows her appearing at number 8 on the bill, followed by Mae, Mack and Marty's high wire act!

NAUGHTON and GOLD, from the Palladium Crazy Gang, in "TO SEE SUCH FUN." NEXT WEEK.

TELEPHONE 2362   Telegrams: "BESTERMS"

THE LEIGH AND DISTRICT
Lending Society, Ltd.
£10 to £1,000 Without Security   13 Cannon Street, Preston

2.—THE EILEEN WINTERTON TRIO
In some novel Tap and Acrobatic Dances.

DEAL WITH OUR ADVERTISERS!

7.—THE EILEEN WINTERTON TRIO
Will entertain you again with some novel dancing.

3.—THE GEDDES BROTHERS
The Musical Scots, they get music out of anything.

STANLEY
CARWIN
LTD.
15a MILLER ARCADE
JACSON STREET
PRESTON
FOR
RADIO
ELECTRICAL
AND
ELECTRO-MEDICAL
EQUIPMENT
Office and Works:
47 CORPORATION ST.
Tel. 5764

8.—The Queen of Comedy
TESSIE O'SHEA
'Nobody Loves a Fat Girl.'

4.—RENEE DYMOTT
The "Unusual" Girl will surprise you.

5.—KITTY MASTERS
Radio's Radiant Songstress in all her latest successes

9.—LESLIE STRANGE
The Famous Radio and Stage Impressionist in some of his latest character studies.

6—INTERVAL   Selection by the Palace Orchestra.

10.—MAE, MACK AND MARTY
In a daring comedy high wire walking speciality.

A BEER IN A THOUSAND FOR THE MILLION

LION ALE

EVERY DROP TIP TOP! BEST IN 1830 —Still the Best

Obtainable at the Bars of This Theatre
LION BREWERY   :   BLACKBURN

NEXT WEEK: NAUGHTON and GOLD, the London Palladium Stars, in "TO SEE SUCH FUN."

staff, which included the now Acting Manager, Ernest Simms. There was the All Star Variety Matinee on Saturday 9 December 1939 in aid of the Mayoress's Comfort Fund and Station buffet, which was a morale boosting programme in those dark times.

In its later years, the theatre orchestra was under the direction of James 'Jimmy' White, and his talented musicians. Billy Seager was principal trumpet for thirteen years, from 1942 up to the theatre's closure. In 1998 I spoke to his widow, Ivy, who is now 82 years-old. She told me about the theatre and how proud she is that her son, Harvey, is carrying on in his father's footsteps, as a resident children's entertainer and multi-instrumentalist at Blackpool Tower.

Billy regularly played a trumpet solo during performance intervals, and at a circus production he told Ivy, 'I have been blowin' my bloomin' brains out all flippin' night for a zebra!'. On another occasion an elephant put its foot down so hard it made a hole in the stage and almost ended up in the band room! Each Monday at 11.30am, a rehearsal of the whole production was performed, and Jimmy co-ordinated his cues from the artists.

One such artist was Jim Tattersall of Little Lever, Bolton. I was privileged when the octogenarian trouper of Britain's music halls granted me an audience, along with his daughter, Heather, at her home in Fulwood. Jim was a past master of his original act of specialised ventriloquism. Tattersall & Jerry played the King's Palace many times and the Royal Hippodrome once, and Jim recalled his life treading the boards and how he hit the big time.

Tattersall & Jerry was an act conceived after Jim left school in Bury and became an engineer for a while at Dobson and Barlows in Bolton. It was here that he developed his ventriloquial and modelmaking skills, which enabled him to construct realistic-looking, life-size dolls with their trade mark 'goggle-eyes'. Apart from Jerry, a naval

Ventriloquist Jim Tattersall with 'The Old Dutch' and her hubby, 'Old Joe'.

puppet friend, there was Old Joe and his dear wife, The Old Dutch, who was propelled across the stage with a Heath Robinson-type elasticised system. During the act when Jim said 'The Old Dutch' that was the cue for Jimmy White in the orchestra pit to strike up with 'We've been together now for forty years', and The Old Dutch would walk across the stage to be serenaded by her beloved Old Joe.

Jim's big break came whilst working the 'bread and butter' circuit at the King's Palace. Following twice-nightly performances, he received a telephone call from the manager of the Winter Gardens, Morccambe, who had been in the audience. The manager told Jim that he was going to London to tell some of his friends about the act. Those friends were Lew and Leslie Grade, and Jim graduated to the Moss Empire circuit of top British theatres. The first of his engagements included the Glasgow Empire, well known for the vitriolic candour and actions of a non-approving audience. He must have been well received when he performed there on a Saturday night, and was brave enough to book a return visit!

Early in his career Tattersall & Jerry got star billing above a comedy duo which were to become the nation's favourite double act, Morecambe & Wise. Jim gets more than a mention in their autobiography and he enlightened me further with his personal recollections. In those days, Eric and Ern did not have a car and, whilst working at the Empire Theatre, Sheffield, asked Jim, 'Where are you working next week?'. 'Edinburgh', came the reply. 'Oh good, can we have a lift and pay half the cost of the petrol?' On another occasion, Eric repaid the favour when he asked, 'Where are you next week?' Jim replied, 'Winter Gardens, Morecambe'. Eric retorted, 'Right, don't book your 'digs', I'll ring my mum up!' Morecambe was, of course, Eric's home town.

Such reciprocal support was common amongst performers, and Jim was to work alongside most of Britain's major stars, including Shirley Bassey, Michael Bentine, Josef Locke, Peter Sellers, Norman Wisdom and Julie Andrews, together with her mother and father, also well-known stage artists. He also performed with the 'King of the Diddymen', Ken Dodd, for whom he made several models.

Jim got his first television break with Eamonn Andrews at the s Theatre, Torquay in 1952. Later in his career, he had his own children's puppet show, *Mr Fixit*, on Scottish Television for three years. He even played the Guild Hall shortly after it opened, before 'putting all his dolls to bed' when he retired in 1975. Jim then took his modelling more seriously and, in 1989, won a silver award for his model of Wigan Pier that was exhibited at the Chelsea Flower Show. The much-admired model village at Haigh Hall, Wigan, is another fine example of his skills. As a lasting tribute to his art, Jim was prominently featured in a television documentary film called *Their Lips are Sealed*, a tribute to ventriloquists of the past.

Recalling his career to me he said, 'It was hard work, especially playing Glasgow Empire on a Friday and Saturday night. There was something magic about the old theatres and those days have gone forever, but it was a fantastic life. I have a lot to thank the King's Palace for, as it gave me the break I was looking for'. Now, sadly, Jim Tattersall, like so many of his contemporaries and his beloved theatres and music halls, has gone forever. Just before he died in January 1999, aged 82, he was working on a model theatre, complete with orchestra pit and working musicians. It could have been a model of the King's Palace, who knows?

Not even Jim, or a very young Julie Andrews, who gave an impromptu performance from the audience one night, could save the Palace from degeneration. A few years later, in 1949, Julie played the Hippodrome, Blackpool, although she had yet to achieve star billing with her rendition of 'Melody of Youth'.

As television began to grasp the nation's attention, the King's Palace played to houses of only twenty to fifty patrons, somehow lost in Broadhead's great vision with capacity for 3,000. An attempt to keep it open with 'girlie shows' simply drove the family audiences away. The end was inevitable and, due to hard times, it closed on Saturday 19 February 1955.

During that last performance, called *Peaches and Screams,* starring one of Jim's best friends, Ted Lune (from ITV's *The Army Game*), Sonny Broadhead went on stage and announced its closure before leaving it to Ted to entertain the audience for an extended show, which lasted until well after midnight. Ted's catchphrase, 'Throw me the keys, I'll lock up!' suddenly took on a particular poignancy for the audience and staff watching this last performance, and who sadly made their home in the early hours.

Down the road the Royal Hippodrome had lost its resident orchestra, following eight years of use by Salberg. It was timely for Jimmy White to transfer most of his musicians, and trumpet-player Billy Seager

The King's Palace Theatre prior to demolition. This was formerly the main entrance in Old Vicarage.
(Lancashire Library, Harris Reference Library, Preston)

The demolition of the King's Palace Theatre in 1964.

gained further employment until the passing of this theatre two years later. The first act the reconvened orchestra accompanied in late 1955 was rising star Shirley Bassey, making her Royal Hippodrome debut. Billy also played at the former Garrick Theatre, Southport, in between bouts of theatre closures.

The King's Palace was the penultimate Broadhead-owned theatre to close, being outlived by the Royal Hippodrome, Salford, by only a few months. The theatrical contents were sold by auction on 17 July 1956, and it stood derelict for eight years before being purchased by a Manchester property developer. After demolition, the Piper Nightclub occupied the site and the late Frankie Vaughan returned to Bishopgate on the same hallowed ground and enthusiastically enlightened his audience about his early appearance at the theatre. Frankie sang all his hits and my wife Dorothy longed for more moonlight, which apparently enticed the master showman!

Epitaph

During its prolonged eight-year stay of execution, it stood forlorn awaiting its fate. I took the opportunity to say hello and goodbye to the embittered warrior by entering the building via an insecure side door. It was cold, dirty, dank and half dark, and an eerie silence prevailed. The red velvet seats and curtains had long been removed, but otherwise it was fully intact. Old theatre programmes were strewn across the dusty dressing room floors, and close by were some steps leading to an open-air balcony directly below the legend 'King's'. It was no doubt a place of private retreat for artists and theatre staff to take a breath of fresh air or, perchance, an opportunity to take a 'quick snifter' before going on stage!

After admiring the proscenium arch, bedecked by marble pillars and flamboyant boxes, I walked up to the stage and looked out at the circle. The faded goddesses could no longer inspire the arts, but seemed to be looking down on me from high above the arch and ceiling. Time to reflect on my childhood and a production called *Dick Turpin Rides Again*, complete with real-life horse. I mused over the formidable roll calls of great and lesser-known music hall stars that once trod the same boards.

I glanced down at the pit and it was almost as though the cold silence was about to be surpassed by the theatre ghost taking its cue. In my mind a final spiritual scenario unfolded. Emerging from the darkest recesses a distinguished gentleman took centre stage. Bright lights now transformed years of decay into a pristine auditorium which again resounded to the clapping of thousands of hands of yesteryear's Prestonians – mums, dads, children with smiling faces, servicemen in uniform – all were out there.

In the pit, the maestro's moustache twitched as the orchestral sounds reverberated, and the cacophony signalled the exit of the maximum capacity audience at the end of the first house, as the safety curtain slowly descended and the musicians played a catchy melody of tunes. Outside in Old Vicarage Lane, a long queue for the second house at nine-o-clock assembled. A rotund man, complete with tuxedo and a broad smile, greeted them as they entered the warm and busy foyer. After money changed hands at the box office, they waited in eager anticipation while the last of the cleaners removed the debris of sweet and cigarette packets from between the plush tip-up seats. An usherette then directed them to their seats and assured them it's a 'reet good show'.

Backstage, some of the 'pro's' had slipped out to the nearest 'boozer'. The stage doorkeeper read *The Lancashire Daily Post* as the artists drifted back, and on stage the flymen scampered back up their ladders. In the bar, the young barman had entertained one of the lady dancers who were now due back on stage. There were not many empty seats left as the safety curtain ascended to reveal apple-green curtains. The stage manager checked the sound settings for the dancers, the maestro took his cue, and it was time to 'ring up the curtain' for the second of the twice-nightly performances. As the house lights started to dim, the image blurred and I found myself back in reality.

Music hall took a long time to die, and I saw all Preston's theatres become dark, then empty and then be removed from the distinguished heritage of the town. From 1955, Britain's towns and cities saw the demise and closure of 150 small and large theatres that could no longer be kept in operation. Principal trumpet-player Billy Seager was so saddened by the King's Palace closure he wrote a poem. It is a fitting epitaph that I reproduce by kind permission of his widow, Ivy:

Farewell to the Palace

Look there my friends at those walls crashing down
Men are at work to build a new town
A new site must grow where the old Palace stood
Look at those bricks and old rotten wood

With its roof caving in great gaps in the walls
I stand here amazed at the fate of these halls
Gone are the days of the joys that they gave
Fate took its hand nothing could save

Yet rubble and dust is not all I see
But beautiful memories so dear to me
Pantos and plays, yes, musicals too
Flash back to memory, I see them in view

Many an artist first played on those boards
Some were just failures while some gained rewards
Names famed today by its henchman TV
May pass by this spot but no Palace will see

Gimmicks unknown though the damn things were there
As I discovered from my music chair

Down in that pit is where I once sat
Charming Dick Whittington and that bloomin' cat

Night after night we played in that pit
Oft feeling sore as there we did sit
Working so hard yet rarely were seen
Only when playing "God Save the Queen"

William Seager

Soft drinks will be served in the interval by our usherettes. Lion Ales are obtainable in the bar of this theatre.

Act Four, Scene One: The Public Hall, 1882–1973

On 22 December 1821 building work commenced on the Corn Exchange, Lune Street, and on 22 September in the following year, the partially completed Corn Exchange, designed by Liverpool architect William Corry, celebrated its first Guild, two years before the completed building was officially opened by the Mayor of Preston. Only the front portion had been built and building operations were suspended whilst the temporary structure adjacent to it housed the Guild festivities. Afterwards the structure was dismantled and the Corn Exchange was opened in June 1824

On either side of the Corn Exchange, the existing attached iron gates once opened onto the butter market. In the centre stood a large grain and vegetable market, adjacent to corn warehouses in Fleet and Wharf Street, close to the trading terminus basin of the Lancaster Canal. This later became the Public Hall auditorium, and has now been demolished. Part of the building was once utilised as a fish market following the removal of the fish stones from the Market Place in 1853, the same year as it was converted into an Exhibition Hall with the construction of a cast-iron and glass roof over its open courtyard.

It has played a major role in historic meetings, provided a backdrop for civic events and trade exhibitions, and a host of famous figures have passed through its portals during an illustrious 150 years. It has also often been at the centre of controversy and election battles. On Saturday 13 August 1842, it witnessed one of the most violent events in Preston's recent history.

The Chartism Movement had encouraged a rally of cotton workers to protest outside the hall against poor wages. The Riot Act was read and the crowds charged. In an attempt to restore order, the mayor, police and soldiers of the 72nd Highlanders stood by in Lune Street, whilst the workers began to throw stones at them. At first, troops fired over the heads of the crowd, who mistakenly believed they were firing blank cartridges. Workers began to throw more stones from the scaffolding outside the hall. The troops shot dead five men and wounded several others. A commemorative sculpture by Gordon Young now stands at the scene, in front of the rebuilt Corn Exchange public house and pedestrian precinct.

The shootings and their aftermath contributed to the longest ever cotton mill strike, which began in 1854 and lasted for thirty-nine weeks. During this time, Charles Dickens became a visitor to the town, reporting on the poverty and hardship so often depicted in his novels including *Hard Times*, which is loosely based on events he witnessed in

Preston. He gave orations in the hall and latterly at the Theatre Royal in 1861, whilst domiciled at the Bull & Royal Hotel, Church Street. If Dickens had been alive in the hungry 1930s, he could have witnessed scenes outside the hall on many Christmas Eves that were truly 'Dickensian'. It could almost have been a production of *Oliver Twist*, with poor and hungry children waiting to receive a meat pie, cake, apple and orange, to provide a little sustenance over the Christmas period.

The escapologist, Houdini, performed great feats when he escaped from the hall on 9 October 1877, only to return again the following evening. Popular touring presentations, such as Sam Topping's Minstrels and William Hamilton's Dioramas, stopped off in 1889 with admission prices between sixpence and two shillings. In addition, there were many private functions such as church tea parties and reunions, and included in the two and sixpence admission was a concert and tea at 6.30 p.m.

In 1882, the building was transformed into a Public Hall with a gallery on three sides to meet the growing demand to provide a centre for musical and public meetings. The opening coincided with Preston Guild celebrations during that year. Indeed the original Corn Exchange and rebuilt Public Hall was the venue for eight Guilds, including three Guild Courts, culminating in the 1972 event.

At the time of its opening, it was the largest public hall in Lancashire, with the capacity for 3,564 – 1,957 downstairs, 807 gallery and up to 800 standing. Latterly seating was reduced to 1,072 downstairs and 726 in the gallery upstairs. The U-shaped gallery was supported by Greek Ionic-style iron columns, fourteen feet apart, rising to impressive arches with an enriched cornice on the capital. Elaborate wrought iron bedecked by a brass railing added the finishing touch to the front of the gallery. Plaster mouldings and sculptured pilasters on walls and ceilings complemented the contrasting decor. Initially, two hundred and thirty gas jets provided the lighting, supplemented by natural daylight, but were eventually replaced by twelve-feet high florescent lamps, that could be lowered by pulleys for cleaning, suspended from the cove ceiling.

Down to earth, the sprung ballroom floor had a special cover that was laid at the time of meetings, fairs and during other multipurpose use. Centre stage was one of the largest organs ever built by Wilkinsons of Kendal. It was installed as a gift and its brass plaque said, 'This organ was presented by local coal merchant, John Dewhurst & Son, to the Mayor, Aldermen and Burgesses of Preston in the Guild Year, 1882. For the promotion and encouragement of a higher musical taste amongst his fellow townsmen, and for the free use of the Preston Choral Society'. This society, founded in 1819, had no fewer than three hundred and fifty members and gave its first concert in the Corn Exchange in 1840.

Barges brought the organ from Kendal on the Lancaster Canal, and with 3,673 pipes and 66 draw stops, it had more pipes than my dad! The mysteries of the water-powered hydraulic engine that 'drove the beast' were pondered by James Tomlinson, the official organist from the date of installation. Recitals took place on Thursday and Saturday evenings and admission was three pence. After his death in December 1927, aged 77, there was no official successor and the organ gradually fell into disrepair. It broke down permanently in 1939, and this fine example of Victorian organ building was never used again whilst at that venue.

In 1882, there were ceremonies for the opening of the hall and the Guild Inaugural Ball was celebrated in the evening. Attended by four hundred and twenty-seven ladies and gentlemen, it was recorded as a 'genial and enjoyable affair'. The following Tuesday evening, Prestonians had the first opportunity to judge the acoustics when the new organ accompanied distinguished soloists and two hundred and thirty members of Preston Choral Society in a performance of Mendelssohn's *Elijah*.

Captain Samuel Norwood and his family organised musical concerts for many years was acknowledged by the local press following the retirement of the Captain on 30 March 1933: 'Preston says farewell to the Norwood Celebrity Concerts tonight. For sixty-six years they have been the events of Preston's musical life. Through their medium, the town has welcomed the great artists of the day. Now they are at an end and Captain Samuel Norwood, who took over after his father, is retiring from business.' Preston's early impresario arranged five concerts a season and, like the Royal Liverpool Philharmonic Orchestra's season at the present Guild Hall, most families bought a season ticket. The Norwood concerts were great social occasions and the list of famous celebrities was breathtaking. The Captain entertained the artists to dinner at the Park Hotel, above Miller Park, where they stayed the night.

Wealthy families in full evening dress went to the concerts by hired coach, and alighted under the Public Hall's great glass canopy. Others had to endure the discomfort of sitting on wooden planks as only the expensive seats were padded with a long cushion. Often the management had to put up the 'house full' signs. The organ was at the centre of the hall's great cultural past and it accompanied some of the greatest *maestri* soloists, choirs and instrumentalists of all time. Serious autograph hunters could have had a field day but the practice was not current within the polite society of the day.

The wealth of talent included Albert Coates, Ben Davis, Rafael Kubelik, Edward Lloyd, Benno Moiseiwitch, Ignacy Paderewski, Anna Pavlova, Anton Rubinstein and Charles Santley. Maud Allen performed her notorious *Salome* dance and, in complete contrast, international soloists included pianists Myra Hess, Solomon, the great Chopin exponent, Lev Pouishnov, and violinist Fritz Kreisler. The Russian pianist, Vladimir Pachmann, turned to his audience and in broken English said, 'Ah you clap – me go wrong – I show you', and played the whole piece again! Vocalists from the hall of fame included Clara Butt and Nellie Melba, the legendary Paul Robeson and Tetrazzini, who 'brought the house down' with an encore of 'The Last Rose of Summer'. The post-World War I period didn't stop German soprano Elisabeth Schumann 'breaking the ice' whilst singing to a rather tense audience in 1921.

For the Guild of 1922, the Hallé Orchestra gave a performance of Parry's *Pied Piper of Hamelin*, with vocalists Peter Dawson and Madame Olga Haley. The orchestra was under the baton of Sir Landon Ronald, Principal of the London Guild Hall School of Music and a composer and a conductor of great repute. Preston Corporation had planned to engage Sir Edward Elgar to conduct the concert but were discouraged by his high fee. During the hall's golden years, William Mengelberg, who made the Amsterdam Concertgebouw Orchestra one of the finest in Europe, appeared before openly declaring his sympathy with the Nazi Party during World War II.

Going back to 1901, the Evangelical Free Church Council of Preston held a United Memorial Service on Saturday 2 February in memory of 'Our beloved Queen Victoria who passed to her reward on Tuesday 22 January 1901 at half past six p.m.' The service included hymns said to be special to the Queen including 'O God our Help in Ages Past' and 'Rock of Ages'.

The 19th of December 1903 heralded the coming of cinema to Preston when a Grand Cinematograph Entertainments was held in the Assembly Rooms. In October of the following year, there was 'The Continental Bioscope' showing 4,000 animated pictures of the Far East, with an admission price of 6d. On 3 March 1910, for a brief season, a large attendance witnessed a cinematography display, *Mad Woman of the Ruined Castle* presented by Henry Hibbert, with Arthur Northop as manager. Programme diversity also featured John Philip Sousa with sixty performers on his farewell tour on 2 February 1911, and Sir Robert Baden-Powell attended a film show on scout life sixteen days later.

Social and public meetings were held at the hall to propagate the town's political and social fabric – limited to men only in those days of politically incorrect chauvinism. The growing Temperance Movement had its Golden Jubilee of Teetotalism. On 15 October 1913, the more militant members of the Suffragettes' Movement gate-crashed a meeting and tied themselves to seats. The stage was a platform for every Prime Minister and politician of note, including Winston Churchill, who addressed the all-male audience in 1913. Clement Attlee, Edward Heath, Harold Macmillan and Harold Wilson also appeared in later years. In 1914, the hall was in use as a recruiting base for young Prestonians prior to their despatch to World War I, and was used for war purposes again during the Second World War.

In the 1940s, the hall's frontage was used as a livestock market with cats, dogs, ducks, pigs, rabbits, and general produce, all available for sale in a serene setting outside the distinctive façade. On Saturday mornings, farmers' wives brought their produce – home-churned butter, free-range eggs, jams from farm-picked fruits, lemon cheese, chives, parsley mint and muffins – and displayed it on the flagstones outside the hall. There were bunches of garden flowers in season, and even pampas grass in the autumn.

One lady who had a stall there was driven by her husband in a pony-trap down Lune Street, which had sets, like most of the streets at the time. The pony missed its footing, pitched forward, and the woman shot out of the trap, landing face downwards in the gutter. Like most women in those days, she wore open 'drawers', known as 'hambags' – one on each leg – and her skirt went up over her head. Her husband was too busy quietening the pony to bother about his wife's predicament. But a gentleman walking up Lune Street, with great presence of mind, whipped off his top hat and placed it in a strategic position. The usual band of loafers began to gather, and the gentleman tried to send them off. 'Get away you idle lot', he said. 'Have you never seen a woman's backside before?' 'Ay', said a man, 'many a time, but we never see'd one wearin' a top hat afore!' Come to think of it, it made a change from plucked naked roosters hanging from their gibbets and added to the colourful scene of the Saturday market!

The large glass canopy, which previously stretched along the Fleet Street side of the hall and round to the front entrance, where it rose to an impressive dome, eventually had to be demolished following several vehicular collisions with the structure. I am told that in the 1950s a runaway bus once gained momentum on the adjacent Lune Street incline. After it had collided with the structure, it was difficult to put back the pieces.

Maestro orchestral conductors mounting the podium were household names. In the 1950s-60s, I got my first real taste of classical music whilst watching Sir John Barbirolli and Sir Charles Groves conduct their respective Hallé and Royal Liverpool Philharmonic orchestras. Whilst standing

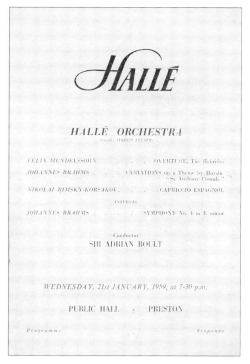

Adrian Boult programme from 1959.

on the gallery promenade in the permitted areas, it was difficult to ignore the sounds of traffic permeating the hall, especially in the quiet musical passages. Sir Thomas Beecham probably thought the same and, known for his candour, he once addressed his Preston audience as a crowd.

Surprisingly, it would seem that locally-born and gifted contralto Kathleen Ferrier, never sang at the hall. Following her meteoric rise to fame, Kathleen's career was cut short when she died prematurely of cancer in 1953. The Preston Cecilian Choral Society and the Preston Symphony Orchestra (which later evolved as the Preston Opera Orchestra) staged huge productions with a large chorus of local singers and internationally-known soloists. The Society was founded in 1927, two years after the old Preston Choral Society was disbanded.

On 25 March 1954, two Preston sporting legends, England and Preston North End player, Tom Finney, and British Middleweight Boxing Champion, Johnny Sullivan, were both in the auditorium at the Mayoress' Charity Ball. Top of the bill was the world-famous Prestonian 'man

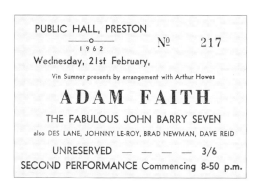

Adam Faith ticket

VIN SUMNER *presents*

Cyril Stapleton's SHOWBAND SHOW

PROGRAMME
ONE SHILLING

A 1950s programme for Cyril Stapleton and his Showband show, presented by Vin Sumner

with the golden trumpet', Eddie Calvert, playing his theme tune 'Oh, Mein Papa', which had just reached number one in the record hit parade. However, the beat of the music was changing, and rock 'n' roll dominated in the late 1950s, as a young Cliff Richard and Adam Faith gave the next generation 'Living Doll' and 'What Do You Want (If You Don't Want Money)'. Needless to say the two young stars got plenty of the latter!

This was the 'Hi-de-hi' era of summer holiday camps, and a young comic had learned a thing or two as a Butlins Redcoat when he played at the hall. Des O'Connor presented a pleasant blend of mirth interspersed with his musical hits – and implied Eric Morecambe misses! Vin Sumner was the man who promoted all these and many more acts, having experienced previous promotions at the Ritz Cinema, Queen's Hall, and Top Rank Ballroom. This was also the era of dance bands, and many a Preston couple took their first steps towards the altar after meeting through Vin at the Public and Queen's halls.

The lack of proper theatrical and stage facilities did not prevent great show business personalities performing, mainly 'one night stands', in the 1960s, and Vin's greatest *coup de grace* was yet to come. If Cliff Richard was being groomed for stardom, then so were the Beatles, an up-and-coming pop group from Liverpool. The biggest-ever UK group played the hall in 1962 and the following year. 'Imagine,' they had been booked for the August 1962 Preston Grasshoppers Rugby Club Dance, and received just eighteen pounds in total courtesy of Vin Sumner.

The Beatles were soon on the road to international fame when, during the same year, they went into Abbey Road Studios, London, to record their first single 'Love Me Do'. The following year Brian Epstein, the Beatles' manager, rang Vin wanting to stage a second concert in the hall. Things were a lot different by now as Vin was manager at the Top Rank Ballroom, and the Beatles were considered far too big for that venue. Indeed, they had been number one in the record charts with both 'Please Please Me' and 'From Me to You'. This presented a dilemma for Vin, as an employee of the Rank Organisation, in promoting a concert at another Preston venue. Fortunately he had never been afraid of making decisions, and so he contracted to go 50:50 on the promotion with Brian Epstein, and present the concert in Vin's wife's name, Alice. The rest is history, as the group appeared at the Public Hall on Friday 13 September 1963 – not unlucky for some, perhaps?

Before the concert, the group had to change their clothes in a van that was being driven around the town centre. When they arrived at the stage door they were able to walk directly on stage, facing 2,000 screaming fans, each of whom had paid 6/- for admission. The teenagers, most of whom will now have families of their own, witnessed a phenomenon and must have warm memories of the 'four lads from Liverpool' live in Preston. Vin Sumner wishes he had retained a few souvenirs of the event, as any Beatles memorabilia is worth a fortune, so hang onto them! The group then had a meteoric rise to fame and, in later years when the Beatles split up, Paul McCartney returned to the town to play the Guild Hall with his new band, Wings.

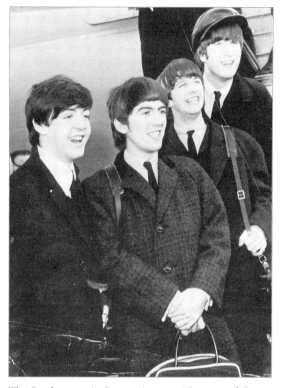

The Beatles were in Preston in 1963. (Courtesy of the *Lancashire Evening Post*)

The hall evokes many memories, but not even the great boxing names that fought there, including Johnny Sullivan and Randolph Turpin, could have saved the auditorium in its final round. The unique maple-wood floor, which once resounded to the sounds of Fats Domino, the Ink Spots and the Glenn Miller Orchestra (directed by Ray McKinley), was soon to be removed, and past generations of happy music lovers would now savour one final performance. After a century-and-a-half of full and varied service to the arts, sports and civic pageantry, it was appropriate that band leader Joe Loss closed it down on 31 March 1973 with a farewell dance, when everyone sang 'Auld Lang Syne'.

During the 1960s, it had been decided to build a new civic hall that would be partly funded by a compensation payout of £1,000,000 from the Ministry of Transport. The payment was for the proposed demolition of the Public Hall which was necessary for the construction of Preston's inner ring road.

The Guild Hall complex, incorporating a concert hall, theatre, restaurant and function rooms, was planned to be ready for the 1972 Guild. An exciting list of artists and events were booked but, owing to industrial action by the builders, the new complex was not completed in time for the historic Guild, and all events were quickly transferred to the grade II listed Public Hall. Personal recollections of that Guild include Saturday night with the Hallé Orchestra, conducted by James Loughran; Sunday's nostalgic concert with Vera Lynn, the famous World War II singer; and all the pomp and

Glenn Miller Orchestra ticket. To dispel any illusion that Major Glenn Miller had arisen from his watery grave to play the hall, it should be noted that the orchestra was under the direction of Ray McKinley at the time.

A ticket from 1961 for Chris Barber & His Jazz Band at the Public Hall 1961. Both this and the Glenn Miller Band in 1958 were promoted by Vin Sumner. In its hey day the Public Hall was able to attract top calibre stars like this.

ceremony of the Guild Court which took place in the large auditorium, with ten handsome coats of arms on either side. Throughout the 1972 Guild, the Public Hall played a major part in these events and it seemed ironic that the building should end as it began in 1822, playing host to a Guild.

After the 1972 Guild, the Public Hall remained in use until 31 May 1973. Shortly afterwards, part of the building was saved from demolition by a member of the public, who was quick to recognise the importance of the Georgian architecture and sent four photographs to the Secretary of State for the Environment at the time, Michael Heseltine. A preservation order proved to be somewhat temporary, however, and over the next seventeen years it was the subject of considerable legal wrangling. Various uses were contemplated for the building, including a radio station and a night club, but none came to fruition.

The Public Hall was purchased from Preston Borough Council by Lancashire County

Petitions to save the Public Hall. (Courtesy of the *Lancashire Evening Post*)

A final dance as Preston says goodbye to the Public Hall, May 1973. (Courtesy of the *Lancashire Evening Post*)

The interior of the Public Hall before demolition. (Courtesy of the *Lancashire Evening Post*)

Council in 1985, who negotiated further with the government over its future. The following year, Conservative minister Nicholas Ridley, who succeeded Michael Heseltine, 'washed his hands' of the matter and announced a change of government ruling. Concerned members of Preston & South Ribble Civic Trust, the Victorian Society and many townsfolk, learned there would be no further public enquiry. Eventually, a so-called compromise was reached which retained the restored front elevation, which was to be known by its original name, the Corn Exchange. Meanwhile, the rear portion, now dry-rot-ridden, was demolished in 1990-91 to make way for improvements to the inner ring road. An inscription over the Wharf Street entrance read 'Erected 1824' and, as it came crumbling down, an opportunity to preserve some of the town's historical identity was lost forever.

After seventeen years of idleness, degradation and prevarication, the hall was ignominiously stripped and Preston's civic pride dented, as the auditorium was demolished. The heraldic Guild Coat of Arms, fine suspended Edwardian lamps, and many other artifacts, were preserved and probably sold to foreign markets. Preston & District Organists' Association wanted to save the organ and experts were called in. But it was disassembled over a four-week period, packed onto a couple of lorries, and taken to a

Demolition of the Public Hall. (Courtesy of the *Lancashire Evening Post*)

redundant church in Halifax, West Yorkshire, which planned to restore the organ at a cost of about £200,000, and use it for recitals on the other side of the Pennines.

All that now remains of the original hall of architectural merit is the Georgian red brick façade, bedecked with a pediment clock tower and cupola, and the town's coat of arms in stone which was originally part of Preston's 18th-century Town Hall. The original plaque, commemorating the opening of the Corn Exchange, is still above the door of the entrance to the hall, which is now just another town centre pub. It reads as follows:

> Corn Exchange
> Erected by the Corporation MDCCCXXII
> Nicholas Grimshaw Esq. Mayor

Over this a later insertion reads

> Enlarged and Restored MDCCCLXXXII
> Edmund Birley Esq. Mayor

Patrons are asked to assist management by following the directions on tickets and occupying the seat indicated thereon with the least possible delay

Act Four, Scene Two
The Guild Hall Entertainments
Complex (1972—)

On 3 July 1970, Preston Council's vision for a prestigious concert hall and theatre finally became reality, when the Ministry of Housing & Local Government informed the Finance Chairman of Preston Corporation that work could start on the £1,806,573 development. The original cost of the complex escalated to £2,170,000, on top of the £380,000 for the land it stands on. Following the Public Hall's temporary reprieve the due million pound payment from the Ministry of Transport was not to be met by way of compensation. However, the town now has an entertainment complex that has proved to be a good investment, and is now worth far more than its construction costs.

It seemed that news of the governmment's agreement to the scheme had come just in time. It was anticipated that there would be two years' construction in order for the building to be ready in time for the 1972 Preston Guild. It was built on an historic central site at Ward's End, a narrow passage leading to the old bus station. Today, the Guild Hall Arcade follows almost the same route, through a subway, to the new bus station. At first the contractor's signs referred to it as the Civic Hall, until it was decided that the obvious name for the whole complex was the Guild Hall. The town has a long tradition of opening new venues for its Guilds, as witnessed by the openings of the Public Hall, Theatre Royal and the humble Guild Cinema, as well as the Guild Hall. The twenty-year cycle of Preston's Guilds has only been interrupted when World War II curtailed the 1942 Guild. In September 1952, the Guild Mayor, Alderman John James Ward, restored the Guild celebrations at the old Public Hall.

It was envisaged that the new Guild Hall would have a major part to play in the pageantry and sitting of the 1972 Guild Court, the proceedings of which form part of the town's Charter, so the complex's theatre was aptly named the Charter Theatre. The contractors were expected to fulfil their obligations and hand over the building on time. During construction hundreds of scaffolding poles appeared to hold the roof up as the futuristic dominant frontage began to emerge on Lancaster Road. There were those who jibed 'the space ship has landed', referring to the design features of the octagonal building standing cantilever-style and in marked contrast to the magnificent Grade I listed Harris Museum and Art Gallery opposite.

The advance publicity had dubbed it the most modern entertainment complex in the north of England. It soon became apparent that modern architecture aimed to accentuate the structural features of handsome brickwork, and a preponderance of glass and sturdy concrete beams were all clearly visible throughout the three-storey building.

As the deadline approached, an anxious public began to ask, 'will it, or won't it, be ready on time'? Anticipation fizzled out completely when a tactical strike by the building workers meant that the opening of the main auditorium was delayed until well after Guild Week, and this was despite special pleas to unions to release the building from the strike.

On 9 August 1972, it was reported in *The Lancashire Evening Post* that the showpiece building was still strike-bound, only weeks from completion. A special Guild Emergency Sub-Committee at the Town Hall took the inevitable decision to plan the celebrations without it. At the time there was a real sense of civic tragedy as Preston Guilds do not come round too often, and to postpone it was unthinkable.

Preston Town Clerk, William Lockley, said after the Sub-Committee meeting, 'This is not going to wreck the Guild. Preston Guild can outlive this sort of trouble that, given good weather, everyone will enjoy themselves, and the fact that we have been denied use of the Guild Hall will only be a pleasure deferred. Whatever happens now the Guild Hall will not be used. We have a commitment to the artists and performers. They have been very understanding of the position and have agreed to leave the final decision until today, in many cases at considerable inconvenience to themselves. We are very grateful to them for their forbearance. Now we simply cannot wait any longer without letting them know where they stand'.

The cliff-hanger resulted in a revised programme, or re-arranged events, which involved postponements, cancellations and transfers to the Public Hall in September that year:

Saturday 2nd:	The third Saturday, and final, proclamation was made at noon followed by a Guild Mayoral Luncheon in the Public Hall
Monday 4th	Public Hall: (Morn), Guild Court Public Hall(Eve) Guild Inaugural Ball with Syd Lawrence & His Orchestra
Tuesday 5th	Guild Hall: Royal Liverpool Philharmonic Orchestra (postponed) Public Hall: (Eve) Old Time Ball featuring Sydney Thompson & His Orchestra
Wednesday 6th	Guild Hall: The Spinners concert (postponed until 12 September) Public Hall: (Eve)Guild Mayoral Ball with Cyril Stapleton & His Orchestra
Thursday 7th	Guild Hall: Mayoral Reception for overseas ex-Prestonians (to Public Hall) Public Hall: Carnival Ball with Kenny Ball (Pop concert postponed till 13 Sept.)
Friday 8th	Guild Hall: Old Time Music Hall afternoon/evening shows (transferred)

	Public Hall: Mayor & Mayoress & Ladies Procession assembly to be arranged
Saturday 9th	Guild Hall: Hallé Orchestra concert (transferred)
	Public Hall: Assembly Rooms. Lunch for Queen's Lancashire Regiment
Sunday 10th	Public Hall: Vera Lynn concert
Monday 11th	Public Hall: Ed Stewart Junior Disco
Tuesday 12th	Public Hall: The Spinners concert
Wednesday 13th	Public Hall: Mungo Jerry and Gary Glitter pop concert

Following the furore of Guild Week, the building workers eventually went back to work, and the Grand Hall was opened with the Guild Mayor's Charity Ball on 9 November 1972. The first show the following night was *The Little Angels of Korea*, which consisted of sixty to eighty dancers giving a spectacular performance for all the family. The Guild Hall was hailed as an instant success, winning lavish praise from both visiting artists and audiences alike.

The official opening ceremony was performed by Alderman W. Beckett, in the presence of the Mayor and civic dignatories, at noon on 10 May 1973. In the evening there was a Strauss Family Music Concert. The hall was re-named the Lockley Grand Hall in recognition of the late Town Clerk, William Lockley, and a plaque was officially unveiled to honour his name.

The Grand Hall opened with 2,142 retractable seats, providing a multi-purpose venue.

The completed Guild Hall. (Courtesy of the *Lancashire Evening Post*)

Backstage at the Charter Theatre, showing a profusion of ropes and pulleys which operate the scenery and props. (Courtesy of the *Lancashire Evening Post*)

The open stage is in six sections and is height adjustable. Visiting singers, instrumentalists and audiences have commented on the 'interesting and variable acoustics', and there are uninterrupted views of the stage from most parts of the hall. Its commodious foyer has two licensed bars.

The complex, which is on a number of levels, has an escalator and lift to a shopping arcade on the ground floor, which takes patrons to the inner promenade area, where the architects have designed an impressive atrium, culminating in an arched roof. Additionally, outside the building, there is an impressive flight of steps overlooking Lancaster Road that reaches the first floor. On that floor is the foyer entrance to the Grand Hall and a café-bar, and on the floor above are the entrances to the Charter Theatre and Celebrity Restaurant. Also, there is the Avenham Suite on the third floor, offering facilities for functions and conferences.

The Charter Theatre has seating for 780 patrons, 566 in the stalls and 206 in the circle, with bars on each level. The large proscenium stage, fully equipped for the majority of productions that could be performed there, is 36-feet deep, 56-feet wide from wall to wall, and the height of the 'fly' is 48 feet. There is space for a reasonably-sized pit orchestra on a platform that can be lowered or raised according to requirements. The theatre was originally meant to double as a multi-purpose hall and exhibition centre but, as the seats were not retractable, it has proved impractical to change the auditorium for other uses. It has remained a fully-seated venue and the priority was always to re-establish commercial live theatre in the town.

In the 1970s, Preston Film Society persuaded the British Film Institute to make an approach to the Borough Council to turn the theatre into a 'one week in four' cinema. But it decided not to be tempted, despite possible future closure of the remaining cinema in the town centre, as the Council thought it was too restrictive for flexible theatre programming.

On 3 June 1973, nearly 10,000 people took time off from Saturday shopping to go

Bill Simpson in *The Secretary Bird* on 14 June 1976.

on a guided tour of the complex, including its backstage facilities, and a second open day took place in August when the town's first commercial theatre for sixteen years threw open its doors to Prestonians. Robin Bowditch, the first stage manager, counted a thousand visitors in two hours, and favourable comments were made regarding seating and uninterrupted views of the stage. One 81-year-old lady said, 'I think the theatre is beautiful and a credit to Preston'.

The open day boosted the box office for the first theatre production staged in November 1973. Richard Todd, who had opened the ABC Cinema fourteen years earlier, now returned to star in the drama *Murder by Numbers*. That Christmas the first pantomime staged was *Mother Goose* with top TV personality of the time 'dodgy, swingin'' Norman Vaughan, veteran TV and film actor, Sam Kydd, and Tony Wright. Later pantomimes featured TV series *Neighbours* stars, including Guy Pearce, who was to go into films including *The Adventures of Priscilla, Queen of the Desert* and *LA Confidential*.

It took a great deal of time, energy and money to tempt the public away from TV, and the first two years were disheartening times for management and staff. But over the years those TV, stage and film stars were to be seen 'treading the boards', including Roy Barraclough, John Barron, John Bentley, George Cole, Nigel Davenport, Liz Dawn, Michael Denison, Ken Dodd, Shirley Anne Field, Dulcie Gray, USA TV western star Ty Hardin, Sidney James, Jon Pertwee, Pat Phoenix, William Roache, Leonard Rossiter, Bill Simpson, Donald Sinden and many, many more. The audiences gradually increased, and the theatre now has regular patrons and a supporters' group, the Friends of the Charter Theatre.

After its rocky beginning, the Guild Hall was helped to success by Vin Sumner, the Borough Council's first Entertainment & Publicity Officer, from 1972 until his retirement in 1986. Vin reflected on his career when I spoke to him in January 1999. All very encouraging for him was a 1973 show featuring Morecambe & Wise, especially when Eric Morecambe first walked into the Grand Hall during the rehearsal and said to Vin, 'Bloody hell, it's the first time we've played in an aircraft hangar!'. The entertainment supremo used his skills as an entrepreneur to lead his professional staff to achieve heights of ingenuity and innovation. Of his working philosophy he says, 'In my opinion, the ratepayers of Preston are the Directors of the Guild Hall'. A constant headache for any manager is to keep a business in the black, never in the red, and, as has always been the case in entertainment in Preston and elsewhere, it is all about filling theatres or, to use the vernacular, 'bums on seats!'

It is astounding to learn that the Grand Hall was orginally intended to be used for orchestral concerts, school prize days, with only the occasional banquet. Clearly someone on the council had ambitions to build the biggest and most expensive village hall in the world! What a joke – Vin's vision and flair didn't make any provision for 'white elephants' on his entertainment invoices! From the opening, every effort was made to make the complex the leading entertainment venue in the UK. Critics could hardly cite the lack of variety or the level of use, and the Royal seal of approval was given by a visit by Her Majesty The Queen and Prince Philip during the celebration of her Jubilee Year in 1977.

From the televised coverage of *Come Dancing* to the annual season of Royal Liverpool Philharmonic Orchestra concerts, it is difficult to imagine any other venue of its size in the UK presenting a more diverse range of top-class entertainment. Indeed, it has come a long way, as sport was not even mentioned in the original brief, yet it is one of the most well-known venues for the Embassy World Snooker Championships. Like it or loathe it, the Guild Hall was, and is, here in Preston to stay, with something for everyone. As this list shows, the range and calibre of the events hosted by the Guild Hall is remarkable:

Sport:	European Badminton Championships (twice), International Badminton Championships. UK Indoor Bowls, World Bowls, Semi-Final of the British Amateur Boxing Championships, International Darts Championships, World Snooker Championships Qualifying Rounds, International Table Tennis Championships
TV & Radio:	Come Dancing, The Fabulous Fifties, Friday Night is Music Night, Let the Children Sing, Salute to Gershwin, The Spinners, The Swinging Sixties with Gerry Marsden (who held aloft the Liverpool Football Team's prized European Cup and led the audience in his hit 'You'll Never Walk Alone').
Film & Stage stars:	Abba, Russ Abbott, The Animals & Alan Price, Kenny Ball & Acker Bilk, Michael Barrymore, Shirley Bassey, Bay City Rollers, Tony Bennett, Steven Berkoff, Pat Boone, Victor Borge, Jim Bowen, David Bowie, Rory Bremner, Elkie Brooks, Dave Brubeck, Max Bygraves, Cannon & Ball, Jasper Carrott, Linda Carter (TV's *Wonder Woman*), Johnny Cash, Roy Castle, Petula Clark, Richard Clayderman, Leonard Cohen, Billy Connolly, Steve Coogan, Bing Crosby & Rosemary Clooney, Culture Club with Boy George, Paul Daniels, John Dankworth & His Orchestra, Jim Davidson, Alan Davies, Les Dawson, Jack Dee, Barbara Dickson, Sacha Distel, Ken Dodd, Val Doonican, The Dubliners, Duke Ellington & His Orchestra, Ben Elton, Emerson Lake & Palmer, The Everly Brothers, David Essex, Lee Evans, Georgie Fame, James Galway, Genesis & Phil Collins, Georgian State Dancers, Gerry & the Pacemakers, Buddy Greco & His Quartet, Hale & Pace, Bill Haley, Mike Harding, Lenny Henry, Woody Herman & His Orchestra, Harry Hill, The Houghton Weavers, Jools Holland & Squeeze, The Hollies, Bob Hope, Hot Chocolate, Engelbert Humperdinck, Eddie Izzard, The Jackson Five with Michael Jackson, Elton John, Tom Jones, Howard Keel, The Kinks, Cleo Laine, Bonnie Langford, James Last & His Orchestra, Syd Lawrence & His Orchestra, Joe Loss & His Orchestra, Lorna Luft (Judy Garland's daughter), Lulu, Vera Lynn, Humphrey Lyttelton & George Melly, Ralph McTell, Johnny Mathis, Meatloaf,

Yehudi Menuhin, Matt Monro, Morecambe & Wise, John Mortimer, Nana Mouskouri, The Nolans, Rudolf Nureyev, Des O'-Connor, Daniel O'Donnell, Elaine Paige, Billy Pearce, Oscar Peterson, Gene Pitney, The Police & Sting, Andy Prior & His Orchestra, Queen & Freddie Mercury, Red Army of Russia, Buddy Rich & His Orchestra, Cliff Richard & the Shadows, Amanda Roocroft, Demis Roussos, William Rushton & Barry Cryer, Sad Cafe, Lily Savage, Leo Sayer, Neil Sedaka, Helen Shapiro, George Shearing, Brendan Shine, Showaddywaddy, Frank Skinner, Wayne Sleep, David Soul, The Spinners, Rosemary Squires, Alvin Stardust, Freddie Starr, Shakin' Stevens, Rod Stewart & The Faces, Tattersall & Jerry, Jethro Tull, Frankie Valli, Barry White, Roger Whittaker, Wings with Paul & Linda McCartney, Victoria Wood, Klaus Wunderlich, Paul Young, Led Zeppelin.

Vin told me that there is only one 'mega-star' who escaped him over the years, namely 'old blue eyes' himself, Frank Sinatra. Negotiations with his London agent to bring Frank to Preston were proceeding quite well, but a problem occurred with transport logistics in securing a nearby landing strip for the Sinatra jet plane. Somebody must have decided that the top level of the bus station car park was definitely not a suitable place to land the jet, and the invitation to 'Come Fly With Me' was never accepted.

Spotlight on the Bing Crosby Concert

If Frank and his entourage didn't want to come up north, one of his great USA contemporaries, Bing Crosby, certainly did. In contrast to the razzamatazz of Frank's requirements, the 'old groaner' simply alighted from a train at Preston Station on a Thursday afternoon in September 1977. Together with other members of the concert, he ambled from the platform to the station approach road, and was conveyed to the Guild Hall for the one-evening performance.

The concert was Bing's only UK performance, prior to his London Palladium appearance, before he suffered a fatal heart attack on a Spanish golf course on 17 October 1977. My greatest mistake was not being at the Preston concert, which also featured Bing's wife, Kathy, and son, Harry, with Rosemary Clooney and Joey Buchkin, plus the UK's favourite warm-up comic at that time, Ted Rogers. It was a concert unparalleled in the Guild Hall's history, with a capacity audience paying £7.50 a ticket, to see the 73-year-old legendary performer sing all, or part, of fifty songs culminating in 'White Christmas'. At the end of the three-hour show, the audience leapt to their feet and gave an unprecedented six-minute standing ovation. I am reliably informed that during Bing's performances the atmosphere was electric, with the 'old magic' prompting more than a few tears from the spellbound audience.

Vin Sumner still regards the concert as the most successful coup of his show business career, and I asked him to reflect on that night:

Bing Crosby on Preston Rail Station. (Courtesy of the *Lancashire Evening Post*)

On this day, entertainment history was made in Preston. At 5.15pm, the London train arrived at Preston Station carrying a living legend of show business. Stepping off the train onto platform six, Bing Crosby appeared along with other members of his fabulous show. Several limousines were waiting to take the party to the Guild Hall, where they were greeted by myself.

Once settled in at the venue, Bing came out into the Grand Hall to watch and listen to the orchestra rehearsing. He sat in the tiered seating of 'B' block chatting to me and other management, including my deputy, Alan Baker, and the conversation was pleasant, very friendly, and to us mere mortals, fantastic! Also, arrangements had been made for an extra special buffet meal for Bing and his party including the orchestra and, although typical of the wonderful person he was, his thoughts were to ensure that all the members of the show were looked after.

The concert started at 8.00pm, and with a 2,142 audience holding its breath, the house lights were dimmed, the orchestra boldly went into Bing's famous signature tune "When the Blue of the Night", and in a white, bright spotlight,

Bing Crosby at the Guild Hall in 1977. (Courtesy of the *Lancashire Evening Post*)

moving onto the stage, was the legend himself. Dressed in an ordinary tuxedo, small in stature, singing as only Bing could, he suddenly appeared and the entire audience greeted him with a standing ovation. Never in my life have I experienced so thrilling a moment, and the comments of the entire audience have supported that statement. History had been made, and the concert, lasting two hours and ten minutes, was out of this world. So often since then, have I heard the words 'I wish I had been there' from so many, many members of the public.

The Guild Hall was now established as a major regional centre for the arts and entertainment and, on Vin Sumner's retirement, a banquet was organised for him and his wife, Alice, in the aptly-named Celebrity Restaurant. With representatives from show business, the Royal Liverpool Philharmonic Orchestra and the world of sport dining there, the restaurant has really lived up to its name.

Michael Johnson was appointed the General Manager in 1986. A former music teacher in a private school, he came from Leeds City Council and had developed the broad music culture there over a number of years. At Preston he brought a wider musical spectrum to the complex, with lesser-known European orchestras and soloists, which proved to be expensive and unfortunately, the expenditure far exceeded the income. However, Michael was successful in persuading Preston Film Society, which was re-formed in 1970 by Bob Higson and Michael Lockwood, to join forces with them to show films with the newly-installed 35mm projection equipment at the Charter Theatre. Full houses were received for *Amadeus* and *Room with a View* and, since the Odeon was the only cinema left in the town, attendance for most Sunday-night-only films were good. Michael was attracted by other challenges at other venues in other towns and left the complex within two years.

The manager of the renowned Grand Theatre, Blackpool, John Shedwick, was appointed his successor, and together with his deputy, Alan Baker, has brought a wealth of theatrical experience to the complex, which has put Preston on the map, especially with continuing live TV transmissions of sporting events. The challenge for the town is to retain all these events and to gain new ones, as they have brought additional trade to the area. Increased competition from newer complexes may make it difficult to use the Hall most cost effectively and to capacity, especially as they seat 10,000 people or more and it is very difficult to attract the very big artists unless a large number of tickets can be sold.

One local tradesman who has no problem at all capitalising on the number of artists and sporting personalities performing at the complex is Joe Swarbrick, the proprietor of the Tea Bar, Lancaster Road. The Tea Bar has a gallery on its walls of the stars who regularly sample the cuisine. Joe told me, 'Roy Barraclough was instantly recognised

Vin Sumner 'bows out', with actor William Roache and his wife, Sarah. (Courtesy of the *Lancashire Evening Post*)

the moment he walked in. He commented on how pleased he was to see the Tea Bar still serving sandwiches after all these years. As a young lad, he remembered working on his parent's Preston market stall, and how he spent most of his days going to the Tea Bar, to collect food for the market traders'.

Joe had many more tales to tell, including one concerning Christopher Beeney, the TV star of *Upstairs Downstairs*, and *In Loving Memory* with Thora Hird: 'He was appearing in *Boeing Boeing* and confessed to being a do-it-yourself fanatic, and gained a City & Guilds Certificate in plumbing!'. Ian Williams, Adam in TV's Australian sitcom *Neighbours*, appeared in a Christmas pantomime: 'He came into the cafe, during mid-mornings, with other cast members. Out of the blue, Ian's younger brother turned up from Australia and asked if he could have a job! We took him on as a dishwasher whilst his brother was playing to full houses almost next door!'.

'Nigel Davenport, the star of *A Man for All Seasons* and *The Virgin Soldiers*, and of TV's *Howard's Way* and *Trainer*, came in for a corned beef and pickle sandwich during his first day in Preston. After that, he came in every afternoon for the very same sandwich, and got to know some of our regulars, and enjoyed a laugh with them. On the Saturday morning, he said he was moving on with the play, and left us a signed photograph thanking the staff for their hospitality. He was a perfect gentleman'.

Another actor, Hilary Minster, known as Herr Flick in the TV comedy series *'Allo 'Allo*, was appearing in a one-night production: 'He came in at lunchtime, and we didn't recognise him immediately, but as soon as he put on his German accent, as used in the TV series, he was unmistakable!'. Sportsmen too have dined in the cafe: 'Kirk Stevens, the Canadian snooker player, came bouncing in one lunchtime with his entourage. He proceeded to order late breakfasts for everyone, and explained how they wanted their eggs cooked 'Canadian style'. I didn't understand his request, so politely invited him to cook them himself, which he willingly did and with great enthusiasm!'.

Though balancing the books is not a problem for this small businessman, it is another thing entirely when it comes to the economies of funding the arts, both at the complex and throughout Preston. As the late twentieth century draws to a close, the government Culture Minister called for a 'less elitist approach to the arts'. Reductions in state funding meant, in the north for instance, that the Hallé Orchestra had to sell-off some of the 'family silver'! Cultural cut backs may ease financial burdens but do not always preserve standards of excellence and adventurous programming for the die-hard devotees of culture. Perhaps the mix should be aimed at a wider audience. There is no need to pay so-called 'elitist' admission charges to enjoy the two main amateur musical societies, Preston Musical Comedy Society and Preston Opera, who perform at the Charter Theatre, attract near-capacity audiences and certainly aim for high professional standards.

Twice a year, the Preston Opera presents productions on a grandiose scale, with a large symphony orchestra. It has developed an excellent reputation, largely due to the professionalism of its members and former Musical Director, Frank Salter. Frank began preliminary planning (which led to his founding of the Opera Group) late in 1964, following post-graduate opera studies in London. After presenting *Don Giovanni* to

Jayne Woollam, a former member of Opera North, as Abigail in Verdi's *Nabucco*.
(Courtesy of the *Lancashire Evening Post*)

The chorus of Hebrew slaves in the same 1992 Guild Hall production.
(Courtesy of the *Lancashire Evening Post*)

the public in 1967, he uninterruptedly held the post of Musical Director until standing down from the podium in 1997. One of its biggest achievements, in recent years, was a lavish 'Opera on the Park', which featured several international soloists, and was held in the open air in Avenham Park for the 1992 Guild. The Royal Liverpool Philharmonic Orchestra and chorus and soloists of Preston Opera were conducted by Frank Salter and Nicholas Smith.

The intrepid nature of the company in staging lesser-known works such as Verdi's *Macbeth* and *Attila*, as well as firm favourites like *La Traviata* and *Carmen*, has earned them an enviable reputation and dedicated patrons. Opera buffs are prepared to travel some distance to witness rare productions, and several members of the company are graduates of the prestigious Royal Northern College of Music, Manchester.

The first opera performed by Preston Opera in the Charter Theatre, when it opened to the public, was Verdi's *Nabucco*; and, during the 1992 Guild, a spectacular production was performed in the Grand Hall. It was the first time that the large hall had been used for grand opera production, and every facet of this major work was performed to perfection, by one hundred and thirty singers from the North West. The one-off performance ensured a capacity audience, and it is hoped to perform another similar large-scale opera in the future. My own recollection of both events is that they were awe inspiring.

Preston Musical Comedy Society presents its own renditions of top musicals and, like Preston Opera, is respected for its dynamic staging of performances by the admirable production team and members. The Guild Hall and Charter Theatre Front-of-House Manager, Eddie Regan, has taken leads in memorable week-long productions of *Fiddler on the Roof*, *Gigi* and *The Sound of Music*. His roots go back a long way to the Empire, Gaumont, Queen's Hall and Royal Hippodrome, when he played roles in other similar productions. His father, Cliff, is also a real veteran of the boards, and a former member.

Opposite: Eddie Regan surrounded by ghosts in the 1998 production of *Fiddler on the Roof*. (Courtesy of the *Lancashire Evening Post*)

A Sort of Musical Marriage
(with the Royal Liverpool Philharmonic Orchestra)

The link between the Liverpool Philharmonic Orchestra and Preston is longstanding, and it would be true to say, using football terms, that a visit to the Guild Hall is not regarded as an away fixture. Prior to World War II, it was rare for orchestras to travel from their home bases. And one assumes that music lovers in Preston had to journey to Manchester to hear the Hallé Orchestra, or to Liverpool for the Philharmonic Society's concerts, conducted by such notables as Thomas Beecham, Adrian Boult or Henry Wood.

In many ways, that war contributed to a revolution in the concert-going habits of the North West. The Liverpool orchestra benefited from an influx of splendid principal players from the London scene, and embarked on a golden era under Malcolm Sargent, this after a valuable holding operation under the unsung Louis Cohen and members of the Merseyside Symphony Orchestra. The orchestra began to make regular visits to Preston, one early instance being in December 1941. The venue was the New Victoria Cinema and the programme included, under the baton of Herbert Menges, a performance of Beethoven's *Emperor Concerto* by Moiseiwitsch.

Royal patronage was not conferred until 1956, and the Liverpool Philharmonic Orchestra as it was known, made frequent appearances throughout the 1950s at the Public Hall. Two significant concerts were those in September 1953 and October 1958, and in the first of these, Gina Bachauer performed the Brahms Second Concerto with Hugo Rignold, and the latter brought together Michael Hambourg and John Pritchard.

The link with Preston strengthened as the number of concerts increased and, by the 1970s, it became necessary to print a separate brochure for concerts at the Guild Hall. A celebratory concert marked the American Bicentenary in 1976, with Charles Groves and a young Peter Donohoe performing works by Bernstein, Gershwin and Ives, and ending with a memorable performance of Dvorak's *New World* Symphony.

Early in the 1980s, it was decided to launch an association of society supporters to be known as the Friends of the Phil, its aim being to lend support to the society in the promotion and performance of national and international music in the region. An important factor in the development of the Friends was the input of the Preston members and particularly Lady Grenfell-Baines. Milena and her colleagues have assumed a major importance within this unique group of music lovers, and have helped to raise the profile of the orchestra to the extent that it now enjoys an international reputation.

Visits to the Guild Hall are looked forward to with pleasure, and the venue is a popular one, and has seen the appearance of many great soloists and conductors.

Following John Pritchard came Charles Groves who directed for fourteen years. The tenures of David Atherton, Marek Janowski and Walter Weller were comparatively brief, but they were followed by Libor Pesek who, like Sir Charles, established a particular rapport with the Preston faithful. Another great favourite was Vernon Hanley, whose interpretations of British music linger in the memory. The musical marriage of the RLPO with Proud Preston has passed the fifty-year mark. Long may it continue to flourish, and Milena will do her utmost to ensure it will.

The marriage between Preston and the Guild Hall looks set to continue. In 1996, the complex was granted over four million pounds from The National Lottery and embarked on a three-year refurbishment programme. Substantial improvements have been made, including refurbishment of public areas and a new heating system. Success has been harnessed by a well-balanced arts programme, including educational events, and a professional marketing policy which has delighted Prestonians, and its patrons from throughout the UK. Its future may change, as national and local politics may change, and it may not remain under the management of the Borough Council. But whoever, or whatever, owns the town's arts, entertainment and sporting complex, Prestonians can be assured of experiencing many more memorable events.

The Guild Hall's 21st Birthday Party. Councillor Peter Rankin, Preston Borough Council's Leisure Committee Chairman, conductor Takuo Yuasa, Lady Grenfell-Baines and pianist Ronan O'Hara.

Encore:

From distinguished actor John Barron

I first met Reginald Salberg in 1948, when he came to see me in a play at the Intimate Theatre, Palmers Green, London. That meeting led to some of the happiest and most enjoyable years that I have known as an actor since I began in the theatre in 1938.

In 1949, I joined Reggie Salberg's repertory Company at the Empire Theatre, Penge, London. Instead of the usual weekly rep., we were to enjoy the great luxury of fortnightly rep., the second week to be played at the Grand Theatre, Croydon. It was a large and splendid company of actors and actresses, among them my future wife, Joan Peart. Some very fine productions were mounted under the direction of Oliver Gordon, but as a whole the season was not a success; the reason being that loyal audiences were upset at only seeing the company once a fortnight instead of every week!

I had, at the time, recently directed a number of plays in rep. at Palmers Green and Leicester, and so I was delighted when Reggie asked my wife and I to join his well-established Company in Preston. The season was to start in January 1951 and

John Barron on stage in *Man and Superman* by George Bernard Shaw at the Royal Hippodrome in 1952.

continue for fifty weeks! At a time of high unemployment in the theatre this was a very welcome offer.

Packing all our belongings we set off for Preston. Joan knew Lancashire well, as she was born and brought up in Manchester. The county was new to me, only having paid a week's visit to Manchester and Liverpool when on tour with a play. After a week in a small hotel in Garstang, we found a splendid flat in a grand house overlooking Avenham Park, and this became our home for two very full and happy years.

The Hippodrome was a fine place to work with plenty of space for backstage activity, and a real theatre with great atmosphere. We were a happy company and many of us had worked together before. I was very pleased to be the director of the plays, and Reggie came up from the South to see us each week, always encouraging us by putting on plays of quality as well as the 'pot-boilers'. Memorable to me were productions of

John Barron, whose work included playing the Dean in BBC television's *All Gas & Gaiters*, and C. J. in *The Fall and Rise of Reggie Perrin* with Leonard Rossiter.

A Streetcar Named Desire (probably the very first rep. production), *T.S. Eliot's The Cocktail Party*, an extravagant week of *The Scarlet Pimpernel*, and the Ben Travers farces were always winners. I was able to keep my hand in as an actor and played regularly often under a guest director. I was greatly helped on the technical side by our stage manager, David Rose, who later was to produce BBC-TV's *Z Cars*, and is now an eminent film producer.

My association with Reggie went on for some time and, after Preston, I was at the New Theatre, Hull and then, for two years, joined his brother, Derek, at the Grand Theatre, Wolverhampton – surely the finest theatre in the Midlands. My days of rep. ended with Reggie once more, in the gentle atmosphere of the cathedral city of Salisbury. The success and prestige of its theatre for many years, was due entirely to Reggie's lifetime of experience in the rep. movement.

The work we all undertook in weekly rep. at the old Hippodrome may, on reflection, seem a bit rough and ready by today's standards, cushioned as companies are by local and government subsidy. In the old days, it was the money taken at the box-office one week that paid for the show the following week!

From renowned local artist Leslie Cant with more memories of the Hippodrome.

It was Reginald Salberg who brought me to Preston and the Hippodrome, where he had recently installed his new Repertory Company. I was glad to be asked, for work at the King's Theatre, Gainsborough was a bit hectic, even for rep. I didn't come for a rest cure, for there is no such thing when you are a member of a company who put on a different play each week. It was the promise that I wouldn't be expected to stage-manage, play parts, or even look after the petty cash!

Painting a new 'set' each week only. That suited me fine. I had been used to doing all the other in addition to, for rep. is about hard work, mucking in and out, as we hopefully inspired our public to imagine, swanning around town and gracing its social life with all the time in the world. The art is to conceal the art, you see! Let your public think it's easy and just comes natural . . .

Well, those days are well past the thirty-year rule, so the truth will out. Sure we enjoyed it. Sure we had affection for 'boards', footlights, prosceniums and safety curtains. A part of the romantic life of theatre that died with the rise of television. A very poor exchange.

Now I look back with wonder! The old Hippodrome, as a workplace, was no better or worse than any other theatre we worked in at that time. The shortages resulting from war, which remained with us years after it was over, resulted in neglect, lack of repair, and making the best of it. I reckon we were good at that.

But Reggie thought that Preston deserved the best, and we all went along with it. As set designer and painter, he sent me to London to purchase a new set of 'flats', door-window-fireplace pieces, rostrums and steps, all made to my own specifications on a unit principle to ring weekly changes with flexibility. Despite shortages, in case you wonder, suffice it to say there were ways and means. Nothing was impossible, just a bit difficult.

But 'flats' were sixteen feet high, and an interior set would have an average perimiter of fifty feet or more to cover with distemper, painted to resemble a half-timbered living room with French windows, stair and gallery, and of course backing to doors and a painted cloth representing a garden, back street, landscape or whatever. Next week might be a penthouse flat with Italianate architectural details, to suggest a gangster's apartment for *On the Spot* ... Next week (Oh! Lord) Shakespeare's *Twelfth Night*. Time off? What's that!

For a while, I persuaded Reggie to get me an assistant, which he did. I guess that's why he thought I wouldn't mind playing small parts for a couple of quid extra. Well, it saves bringing up somebody from London to play a cough-and-a-spit. Who could refuse such a reasonable request?

As you can see, good times depend on good work, good people to work with, and a good audience. Preston and its old Hippodrome gave us all three. It gave me a bonus too. I married a Lancashire lass, brought our kids up and have lived here ever since.

From retired chartered accountant and native of Fulwood, Derek Bee

As a schoolboy in the 1920s, I was taken by my parents to the Empire to see a grand opera, *Tales of Hoffmann*, and Fred Perry and Julia Nielson in *The Scarlet Pimpernel*. They were both fairly old actors and Fred was well past his 'sell-by' date as the youngish Pimpernel! During the 1930s, I saw many performances of the Preston Amateur Operatic Society and I remember, in particular, Flossie Goldberg, whose husband was the proprietor of the Gift House, a fancy goods shop in the Miller Arcade. Also, at that time, I remember the Theatre Royal was a cinema and not a theatre, but it still looked like a theatre with crush rooms, a bar and a very small grand circle.

During the 1930s, I, and three or four of my friends had a night out each Friday to attend one or other of the theatres, or occasionally a billiard hall. We met frequently at the Hippodrome, where we usually took the 'prompt' side stage box, which cost little more than the orchestra stalls. The turns were well-known stand-up comedians, acrobats and singers and, usually, a troupe of dancers although not of the class of the Tiller Girls!

The acts in the printed programme were numbered one onwards, and a lighted panel on each side of the proscenium indicated which turn was to appear next, as they were not always presented in numerical order. If a turn was not to our liking, as soon as the number appeared we adjourned for liquid refreshment in the County Wine Stores, which was situated on Friargate opposite Orchard Street, by which there was a short passage leading to the entrance of the theatre.

We also sometimes visited the Palace and theatres. The manager of the latter was a neighbour of one of our party, and we were sometimes given complimentary tickets. Of the two theatres, the former usually had the better turns, and we saw such artists as Billy Bennett, Max Miller and Ted Ray. On one occasion, Tommy Trinder came down from the stage to the front row of the orchestra stalls, where we were sitting, and asked one of my companions for a cigarette. He handed Tommy a nearly full packet of twenty, passed the packet round to other patrons, and then returned the empty packet back to my friend!

The New Victoria was never to my knowledge a live theatre, although by the time the building was complete, with an orchestra pit and a cinema organ, talking pictures had started and sound equipment had to be installed. I attended its opening *circa* 1930 with a complimentary ticket and there was a full orchestra in the pit. During that decade, cinema attendance was at its highest, and there were barriers at the rear of the ground floor near its entrance, around which one queued, sometimes for as long as twenty or thirty minutes.

I visited many other cinemas and, after I married in 1936, my wife and I attended one or another of them probably twice a week. The Empress was a particular favourite because it was comparatively modern for that time, and there was good car parking. We also enjoyed the Carlton, Guild, Palladium, Ritz and Savoy but our choice was decided solely by where a film we wanted to see was showing. The films in the 1930's were chiefly light-hearted comedies and musicals with stars such as Fred Astaire and Ginger Rogers, Bing Crosby and Janet Gaynor.

When I was serving in the Royal Air Force during World War II, I remember sitting through two continuous showings of Rita Hayworth in *You Were Never Lovelier* in the cool air-conditioned Metro Cinema, Calcutta, to escape the stifling heat in India at the time. After the war, we continued to go to cinemas that were well attended. We often had to queue in the street, except at the New Victoria where, at the back of the stalls, one waited for a seat in an ingenious arrangement of metal barriers, so that one could stand and not miss the opening scenes of the film!

I have attended the UCI Cinema only once, but I was not permitted to smoke my pipe!

Recollections of Saturday cinema clubs by Peter Vickers

In the early 1950s, I was lucky enough to spend Saturday mornings at the G. B. Club, New Victoria Cinema, Preston. We caught the P20 bus from Lostock Hall which delivered my friends and I to the old bus station, with time to look round Merigold's and Mears' toy shops, before joining the other members of the G. B. Club. I frequently had to take a neighbour's small son with me who was troublesome, but then his mother did provide the sixpence to get in and a further sixpence for a choc ice, something my mother could not afford. The programme was made up of short films, cartoon, interest, serials plus of course community singing, a juvenile 'live act' and birthday treats on stage for the lucky ones. The G. B. song went thus:

> *We come along on a Saturday morning, greeting everybody with a smile,*
> *We come along on a Saturday morning, we all think it's well worth while.*
> *As members of the G. B. Club we all intend to be,*
> *Good citizens when we grow up and champions of the free.*

We come along on a Saturday morning greeting everybody with a smi-i-le,
Greeting everybody with a smile.

The road-safety song was set to the tune of Lambeth Walk:

Any evening, any day, any time you're down our way,
You'll find us all doing the Safety Walk.
Halt at the kerb, look left there, right there, left there.
When you see that all is clear, you'll have nothing else to fear,
You'll find us all doing the Safety Walk. Hey!

My cousin was a monitor at the Club, I think they had some privileges but can't remember what they were. As I grew a little older things began to change, perhaps for the benefit of the cinema staff, as I recall that they began showing feature films with *The Overlanders* being the first. This did away with the 'Uncle' aspect of attendance and it became just a picture show.

To rival, or complement, the G. B. Club, there was always the Saturday Matinee at Bamber Bridge Pictures, as it was always known. Then it was quite common to have more than one serial at a show. *Flash Gordon* seemed to run forever, rivalled by *Johnny MacBrown* and *Deadwood Dick*, which must have been repeated as it seemed to be always showing. There were The Three Stooges, and the guy who came out from behind the '8 Ball' and, of course, the Nat King Cole Trio musical shorts.

I remember one special Saturday when I visited not only the G. B. in the morning and Bamber Bridge in the afternoon, but also paid a visit to St Gerard and Our Lady's Church Hall, Lostock Hall in the evening where they had films each Saturday night for a good number of years. Mr. Worcester who had a paint shop in Brownedge Road was the projectionist, and I think he must have used 16mm. film equipment as it had to be stored away each week. The films were always aimed at the family audience.

St James Church Hall, Lostock Hall also had occasional film shows on Saturday nights. A young man called Eddie who lived somewhere near Eldon Street, Preston showed the films. I remember one week when Eddie asked us to his home where he had the front room equipped as a cinema with the beam of light from the projector diverted via two mirrors to lengthen it and so increase the size of the screen. We enjoyed the film in his home, but then I had quite a row with my mother because she insisted that I supported his efforts at St. James's, on the following Saturday night, by watching it again. I, of course, wanted to go to St. Gerard's where they were showing a different film. My mother won the day!

My next encounter with Saturday Matinees was about 1970, when some enthusiastic film projectionist agreed to supplement the bingo at the Empress, Eldon Street by having a Saturday Matinee Show for the children. I was able to attend because I could accompany my two young sons. I enjoyed the films, but it didn't last very long before it became a roller-skating rink. I have often wondered if that projectionist might have been Eddie who lived in that area?

Finally, when our young family had moved back to Preston after our short stay on the Fylde, I was allowed to take my children to the ABC Saturday Morning Matinee, or rather they could take me! You had to have a child to accompany you on such visits. What a contrast to the early 1950's, when children were well behaved, or ejected. Chaos is the word that springs to mind as I look back on the ill-disciplined children who ran about unchecked, not being used to cinema attendance, and taking advantage of any semblance of authority. It had to be a very good film to get them to finally sit down and watch it.

A Celebration of Cinemas & Theatres in Preston

ABC Cinema, Fishergate (1959-82)
Alexander Picture House, Walker Street (closed about 1926)
Bennett's Electric Theatre (later Dominion, then Rex), Cragg's Row, off Moor Lane
Carlton Cinema, Blackpool Road, Ribbleton (1932-61)
Coronation Hall, corner of Waterloo Road and Wellington Road (1913)
Cosy Cinema, St Peter's Street (1921)
Embee Hall (later Pictureland by 1910), 1 Avenham Street
Empire Theatre, Church Street (1911-74)
Empress Cinema, Eldon Street (1929)
Grand Cinema (later Regal, then Lido), corner of Marsh Lane & Bow Lane (1921-59)
Guild Cinema, Geoffrey Street (1922-59)
Guild Hall & Charter Theatre, Lancaster Road (1972)
Imperial Picture Palace, Mill Bank, Church Street (1908)
King's Palace Theatre, Tithebarn Street (1913-55)
Marathon Cinema, 66 Frank Street (1913)
New Victoria (later Gaumont, then Odeon), Fishergate (1928-92)
Palladium Cinema, Church Street (1915-68)
Picturedrome, Brackenbury Place
Picture Palace, corner of Brook Street & Broom Street
Playhouse, Market Street West (1949)
Plaza Cinema, New Hall Lane (1932)
 Theatre, Tithebarn Street (1882-1964)
Public Hall, Lune Street (1882-1973)
Queen's Cinema, (later Continental), Tunbridge Street
Queen's Hall, Walker Street (1940-80's)
Ritz Cinema, Church Street (1937-86)
Royal Hippodrome Theatre, Friargate (1905-57)
Savoy Cinema, Ashton Street (1921-58)
Star Cinema, corner of Corporation Street & Fylde Road (1921-59)
Temperance Hall (later Picture Palace), Elizabeth Street (1908)
Theatre Royal, Fishergate (1802-1955)
Tivoli Cinema, Fleetwood Street (1920-58)
UCI Cinemas, Riversway (1990)
Victory Cinema (later Rialto), St Paul's Road (1920-58)

Warner Cinemas, The Capitol Centre (1991)
Other local cinemas:
Empire, Clayton Street, Bamber Bridge (1910-58)
Hippodrome, Preston Road, Leyland
Lyric, Liverpool Road, Penwortham (1931)
Palace, East Street, Leyland
Palace, Longridge (1912-92)
Regent, School Lane, Leyland
(All the above are now closed except for the Guild Hall, the Playhouse, and the UCI and Warner Brothers cinemas)

A celebration of some of the artists who trod the boards in Preston's lost theatres

Arthur Askey	told jokes to his 'playmates' and ended with 'The Busy Bee' song
Hylda Baker	droll humour with Cynthia, 'She Know's Y'Know!'
Roy Barraclough	Preston's own star of stage and television
Shirley Bassey	'This is My Life'
Billy Bennett	'The League of Nations' spoken patter and monologues
Ivy Benson	and her all female band
Issy Bonn	Jewish humour
Peter Brough	with 'Archie Andrews' and a successful wireless show with his ventriloquist act
Sam Brown	singer
Teddy Brown	xylophone player extraordinary
Albert Burden & Co.	comedians
Clara Butt	contralto singer of Elgar's *Sea Pictures*
Charlie Cairoli	best known clown at Blackpool Tower Circus
Eddie Calvert	Preston's finest trumpeter
Ronnie Carroll	ballad singer
Kay Cavendish	singer
Harry Champion	very fast singer with 'Boiled Beef and Carrots!'
Charlie Chaplin	may have appeared with Fred Karno's Troupe
Charlie Clapham & Bill Dwyer	with jokes including 'Cissy the Cow'
Jimmy Clitheroe	short comedian always dressed as a naughty schoolboy
Coco the Clown	world famous artiste
Billy Cotton & his Orchestra	'Wakey Wakey'

Dante	the wonderful magician
Billy Danvers	Liverpool comedian, 'always merry and bright'
Fats Domino	rock'n'roll with 'My Blue Heaven'
Tommy Dorsey & His Band	the big band sound from the USA
Bunny Doyle	the hilarious pantomime comedian
Percy Edwards	ornithological expressionism (bird songs!) which didn't extend to eating worms!
G.H. Elliott	sang 'The Lily of Laguna'
Dick Emery	'Ooh, you are awful, but I like you'
Arthur English	cockney comedian wearing a wide tie
Norman Evans	'Over the garden wall'
Sid Field	king of revues usually as a 'spiv'
Gracie Fields	'Sally'
Tom Finney	Preston's great soccer hero
Flotsum & Jetsum (Hilliam & McEachern)	pianist and singer with 'Only a Few of Us Left'
Florrie Forde	belted out 'A Long Way to Tipperary'
George Formby Snr. & Jnr.	'Leaning on the Lamp post'
Tom Foy	the country bumpkin and a donkey!
Freddie Frinton	great 'drunken' comedian
Ronald Frankau	'idle rich' comedian
Will Fyffe	'I Belong ta Glasgae'
Gertie Gitana	signed her photos 'It matters not how long you live but how' & sang 'Nellie Dean'
Henry Hall & His Orchestra	'This is Henry Hall on the BBC'
Tommy Handley	the radio ITMA shows
Charles Hawtrey	long before the *Carry On* films
Will Hay	'Good Morning, Boys'
Dicky Henderson Snr. & Jnr.	character and 'gag' comedians
Myra Hess	on the classical piano
Harry Houdini	USA escapologist even Preston tried to capture!
The Ink Spots	'Whispering Grass' from the quartet
Jimmy James	hilarity and usually 'drunk' with cigarette under a street lamp!
Jane	of the Daily Mirror 'showed off some flesh' whilst wearing a body stocking!
Jimmy Jewel	comedian and actor, and the 'other half' of Ben Warriss

Hetty King	Dressed as a male marine smoking a pipe with 'All the Nice Girls Love a Sailor!'
Joe King	'Our House has the Mucky Curtains!'
Eartha Kitt	sang and purred like a cat from her seductive sofa!
Harry Korris	great pierrot and comedian and the 'Falstaff at Blackpool South Pier'
Fritz Kreisler	the famous Austrian violinist
Charlie Kunz	piano syncopation
Lily Langtry	turn of the century actress known as the Jersey Lily
Harry Lauder	'Roamin' in the Gloamin''
Evelyn Laye	musical comedy star of the 1920s-30s
The Two Leslies: Sarony & Holmes	nonsense songs 'I Lift up my Finger and I say Tweet Tweet'
Carroll Levis	talent show searcher and compère extraordinary
Little Tich (Harry Relph)	Four feet tall and able to balance on his long boots!
Marie Lloyd	cockney humour with 'A Little of What You Fancy!'
Josef Locke	sang songs from 'White Horse Inn'
Norman Long	a song, a smile and a piano
Ted Lune	emaciated comedian without teeth!
Nellie Melba	soprano from Melbourne, Australia
Max Miller	'the cheeky chappie'
John Mills	the remarkable character film and TV actor
Albert & Allen Modley	Lancashire 'ditties' with flat caps
Eric Morecambe	and little Ern
Dave Morris	often with Joe Gladwin
Derek Nimmo	actor and raconteur
Ivor Novello	as an actor and producer 'Keep the Home Fires Burning'
Tessie O'Shea	humour and songs with her ukelele
Donald Peers	singer 'By A Babbling Brook'
Sandy Powell	comedian 'Can you hear me mother?'
Frank Randle	comedian 'Get off mi foot!' The air was blue
Ted Ray	fiddling and fooling, humorous stories with a violin
Beryl Reid	comedienne including her Brummy 'Marlene'
Old Mother Riley	hilarious man dressed as old woman!
Paul Robeson	'Old Man River'
George Robey	the 'Prime Minister of mirth'
Leonard Rossiter	stage comic actor who became Rigsby in ITV's *Rising Damp*
Victor Seaforth	with Flanagan & Allen type songs

Tod Slaughter	with outrageous melodramas like *Sweeney Todd*
Solomon	brilliant pianist who began at eight and was paralysed forty-five years on
Randolph Sutton	singing 'Mother Kelly's Doorstep'
Richard Tauber	the operatic tenor 'My Heart & I'
Vesta Tilley	male impersonator
Frankie Vaughan	crooner 'Give Me the Moonlight'
Bill Waddington	Lancashire comedian (aka Percy Sugden of ITV's *Coronation Street*)
Dorothy Ward	usually principal boy in pantomime
Jack Warner	(aka policeman of BBC TV's *Dixon of Dock Green*) and his sisters Gert & Daisy
Western Brothers (Kenneth & George)	in evening dress & monocles 'Keeping Up the Old Traditions'
Jimmy Wheeler	comedian and violinist 'That's yer lot'!
Albert Whelan	immaculate in evening dress singing 'Lüstige Brüder'
Robb Wilton	comedian and usually an incompetent official
Wee Georgie Wood	sentimental humour and like Jimmy Clitheroe
Harry Worth	comedian 'My name's Harry Worth. I don't know why, but there it is'.
Anne Ziegler & Webster Booth	songs from the Ivor Novello musicals

Seventeen Broadhead Halls of Glorious Entertainment – Fourteen theatres & one dance hall built two theatres purchased:

13 April 1896, Royal Osborne, Manchester
11 April 1898, Metropole, Manchester
10 October 1901, Junction Theatre & Floral Hall, Manchester
13 October 1902, Hulme Hippodrome, Manchester
7 March 1904, Hippodrome, Salford
18 April 1904, Quee'ns Park Hippodrome, Manchester
10 October 1904, Hippodrome, Bury
18 November 1904, Empire, Ashton-under-Lyne
16 January 1905, Royal Hippodrome, Preston
16 October 1905, King's, Longsight, Manchester
9 October 1907, Crown, Eccles, Manchester (purchased)
21 February 1908, Pavilion, Liverpool
21 December 1908, Pavilion, Ashton-under-Lyne
4 April 1909, Winter Gardens, Morecambe (purchased)
31 July 1909, Palais-de-Danse, Ashton-under-Lyne

10 November 1912, Empress Electric, Manchester
6 February 1913, King's Palace, Preston

'Thanks for the memory'

The End

Acknowledgements

I wish to acknowledge the valuable help, support and sources of research given by the following:

Roy Barraclough of Greater Manchester

John Barron of Sussex

Derek Bee of Goosnargh

Francis Birkenshaw of Ashton

Jim Bowen of Lancaster

Peter Brown of Penwortham

Major Burt-Briggs of Lytham St Annes

Leslie Cant of Fulwood

Nellie Carbis of Grimsargh

Louise Connell of Harris Museum & Art Gallery, Preston

John Cotterall of Southport, author of *Preston's Palaces of Pleasure*

Sir Bernard de Hoghton of Hoghton Tower

Ann Dennison & staff of Harris Reference Library, Preston

Lady Grenfell-Baines of Preston

Mike Hine of Harrogate

Peter Honri, author of *Working the Halls*

Geoffrey Mellor, author of *The Northern Music Hall*

Eddie Regan of Leyland

Dr. Frank Salter of Fulwood

Stephen Sartin of Fulwood

Doris Scholes of Fulwood

Doris Seger of Bamber Bridge

John Shedwick of Thornton Cleveleys

Ian P. Smith, author of *An Historical Account of Preston Public Hall & Corn Exchange"*

Vin Sumner of Penwortham

Jim Tattersall of Little Lever

Vince Tindal, Hon. Historian of the RLPO

Max Tyler of British Music Hall Society

Peter Vickers of Preston

Susan Wain of Longton

Robert Wilson of Blackburn

Professor Richard Wilson of Lancaster University

author of *Shakespeare and the Jesuits*

published in The Times Literary Supplement of 19 December 1997

Neil Hodkinson (former Editor), Lisa Mault, Jackie Taylor, Louise Turner, Library & Photographic Department, and readers of the *Lancashire Evening Post*, Preston.

Michael Lockwood for his patience in word processing the whole manuscript

Anna Goddard & Alistair Hodge of Carnegie Publishing, Lancaster, for professional expertise & for making it all possible

Theatre Programmes Through the Ages

Theatre ⚜ Royal,

PRESTON.

Friday, February 9th, 1872.

A M A T E U R

Dramatic Performance,

In Aid of the General Funds of the

BLIND INSTITUTE,

Under the Patronage of most of the County NOBILITY & GENTRY

Tickets, Programmes and Plans of the Theatre at Mr NORWOOD'S Music Saloon, Fishergate.

ADMISSION : Dress Circle, Three Shillings. Centre Amphitheatre (Reserved), Two Shillings. Amphitheatre Sides, One Shilling and Sixpence. Pit, One Shilling. Gallery, Sixpence. No Half-price.

The Performance will commence punctually at Half-past Seven, Doors open at Seven.

Carriages to be ordered for Half-past Ten.

[*Turn over for Programme.*]

An early Theatre Royal programme, urging that carriages must be ordered by ten thirty!

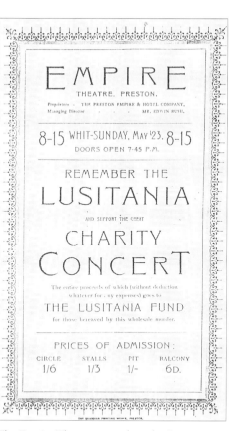

The Empire Theatre remembers the *Lusitania* at a charity concert. The *Lusitania* sank at Kinsale off the south coast of Ireland on 7 May 1915 with the loss of 1198 lives. The Germans, whose U-boat had sunk the vessel, claimed that it was carrying arms, a claim which was later proved to be accurate.

The grand opening night at the Empire on Monday 22 May 1911. (Harris Museum and Art Gallery)

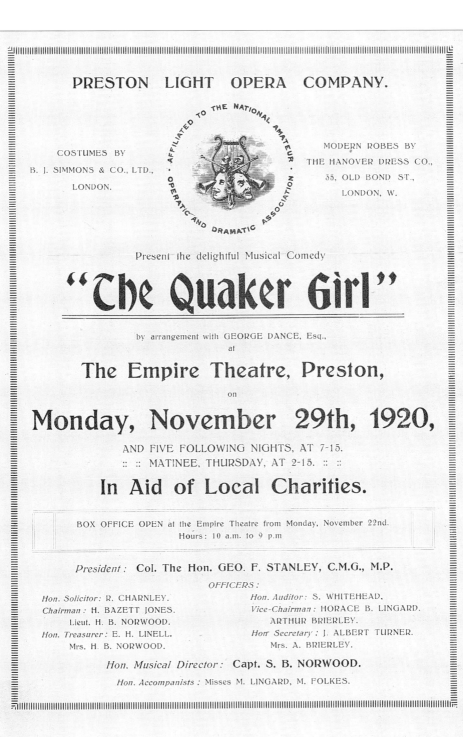

PRESTON LIGHT OPERA COMPANY.

COSTUMES BY
B. J. SIMMONS & CO., LTD.,
LONDON.

AFFILIATED TO THE NATIONAL AMATEUR OPERATIC AND DRAMATIC ASSOCIATION

MODERN ROBES BY
THE HANOVER DRESS CO.,
55, OLD BOND ST.,
LONDON, W.

Present the delightful Musical Comedy

"The Quaker Girl"

by arrangement with GEORGE DANCE, Esq.,
at

The Empire Theatre, Preston,

on

Monday, November 29th, 1920,

AND FIVE FOLLOWING NIGHTS, AT 7-15.
:: :: MATINEE, THURSDAY, AT 2-15. :: ::

In Aid of Local Charities.

BOX OFFICE OPEN at the Empire Theatre from Monday, November 22nd.
Hours: 10 a.m. to 9 p.m

President : **Col. The Hon. GEO. F. STANLEY, C.M.G., M.P.**

OFFICERS :

Hon. Solicitor: R. CHARNLEY.
Chairman : H. BAZETT JONES.
Lieut. H. B. NORWOOD.
Hon. Treasurer: E. H. LINELL.
Mrs. H. B. NORWOOD.

Hon. Auditor: S. WHITEHEAD.
Vice-Chairman : HORACE B. LINGARD.
ARTHUR BRIERLEY.
Hon Secretary : J. ALBERT TURNER.
Mrs. A. BRIERLEY.

Hon. Musical Director: **Capt. S. B. NORWOOD.**

Hon. Accompanists : Misses M. LINGARD, M. FOLKES.

The first page of a stylish programme for a 1920 production of *The Quaker Girl.*

Further Extensions in Cannon Street now open

Everything for everybody all the year round.

Established over a Century.

Frontage in Fishergate and Cannon Street, 77-ft.

Floor Space of Showrooms, together with Stockrooms, Warehouse and Brush Works, is over 14,000 sq. ft.

7 Windows!   7 Stocks!!   7 Departments!!!

For articles required and not on view, please enquire.

The assemblage of goods in each department at 'Xmas always will be larger than in the past.

Established over a Century.

'Xmas Eve, 1920.

Thomas Mears,

Brush Manufacturer and Dealer in Trunks, Bags, Brass, Cabinet, Fancy and Electro-plated Goods.

Toys, Baskets, Woodware, Mats, and Household Requirements.

BRUSHES

SAVE MONEY

REGᴰ TRADE MARK.

14 & 15, Fishergate,
2, 3, & 4, Cannon St., PRESTON.

Telephone 1219.

A typical page of advertisements from *The Quaker Girl* programme.

EMPIRE THEATRE, Preston

MONDAY, NOVEMBER 3rd :: Six Nights at 7.30

MATINEE on THURSDAY at 2.15

PERSONAL VISIT of

Arthur Bourchier

in an Entirely New Production of

HENRY BERNSTEIN'S

Famous Play

THE THIEF

(PRIOR TO STAGING IT ON HIS RETURN TO

THE STRAND THEATRE, LONDON)

with a

SPECIALLY SELECTED COMPANY

including MISS

Kyrle Bellew

JAMES CAREW

STELLA MERVYN-CAMPBELL

The Thief, from the 1920s.

A postcard advertisement for *Treasure Island* at the Empire in 1929.

THE EMPIRE THEATRE - PRESTON.
MONDAY, SEPTEMBER 18th, for Six Nights. Twice Nightly at 6-40 and 8-45.

ANDRE CHARLOT and PAUL MURRAY
PRESENT

THE FAMOUS REVUE

From the . .
VAUDEVILLE THEATRE. LONDON

Cicely Courtneidge

"POT-LUCK"

By RONALD JEANS and DION TITHERADGE. GE.

With the
CELEBRATED LONDON STARS—

Jack Hulbert

CICELY COURTNEIDGE
and . .
JACK HULBERT

Supported by FULL LONDON COMPANY

Chorus and Entire Production
direct ————
from the Vaudeville Theatre

"The Hit of London's Last Season"

This page and opposite, a programme for a 1920s production of *Pot Luck*.

Andre Charlot & Paul Murray's— "POT-LUCK"

The "Pot Luck" Girls

The Egyptian Cigarette in "Cigarette Land"

Jack Hulbert in "The Cure"

The Famous Revue from the Vaudeville Theatre, London, with **Jack Hulbert & Cicely Courtneidge**

John Waddington Ltd., Leeds and London

MONDAY, 15th APRIL 1929

6-40   TWICE NIGHTLY   **8-45**

THOS. F. CONVERY'S ENTERPRISES, LIMITED,

PRESENT, ANOTHER

THOS. F. CONVERY
COMEDY REVUE :

"FORMBY'S NIGHT OUT"

Invented by THOS. F. CONVERY.

Written and Produced by THOS. F. CONVERY and
ARTHUR MERTZ.

SCENE 1 .... **HUNTING SCENE**
John Willie .... GEORGE FORMBY
Dog .... MICKY DRIPPING
Master Ronald .... HARRY CLAYTON
Ted .... HARRY BRENTON
Molly .... LILIAN CONAN

SCENE 2 .... **TABS**
Speciality .... LILIAN CONAN

SCENE 3 .... **THE A.A. STATION**
John Willie .... GEORGE FORMBY
Dog .... MICKY DRIPPING
A.A. Man .... HARRY BRENTON
Dude .... ROBERT OLRAC
Girl .... LILIAN CONAN
Fireman .... JACK OLRAC
Bully .... HARRY BRENTON
Policeman .... JACK OLRAC

SCENE 4 .... **TABS**
Stretcher Bearers ... HARRY CLAYTON and
B. MORRIS

TEA OR COFFEE WITH BISCUITS, 6d

may be had at the Intervals. Use this

EXCHA
PURC

YOU

Preston

Our Supe
Corporati
out doubt
in

Let Servi
Yo

NEXT W
6-40 TW

The Famou

CO-OI

In a N

Call, W
Box Office o

NGE,

ASE, or

SERVICE

CAR AT

GARAGES LTD

emier Motor
pot

rvice Station,
Street, is with-
e of the finest
gland.

Decide
Purchase !

ATTRACTION
NIGHTLY   8-45

A "Company of

HE
TIMISTS

Programme .

or Phone 533.
o a.m. to 9 p.m.

SCENE 5	THE HOSPITAL
John Willie	GEORGE FORMBY
Dog	MICKY DRIPPING
Matron	PAULINE OLRAC
Nurse	LILIAN CONAN
Warder	JOHN OLRAC
Nippy	ROBERT OLRAC
A Reverend Visitor	HARRY BRENTON
Speciality	THE OLRACS

SCENE 6	THE NIGHT OUT
John Willie	GEORGE FORMBY
M.C.	HARRY BRENTON
An Assistant	LILIAN CONAN
Commissionaire	JOHN OLRAC
Another Assistant	DORA YEATES
T. OLRAC	B. OLRAC	F. OLRAC
Song	HARRY CLAYTON
Song	LILIAN CONAN

SCENE 7	TABS
Song	HARRY CLAYTON

SCENE 8	THE VOYAGE
John Willie	GEORGE FORMBY
The Officer	HARRY BRENTON
Dance	GRAINGER GIRLS

SCENE 9	TABS
Comedy Dance	JIMMIE HARRISON

SCENE 10	TABS
Speciality	GRAINGER GIRLS

SCENE 11	THE PALACE
Speciality	GEORGE FORMBY
And Full Company	FINALE

Governing Director	THOS. F. CONVERY
Manager	LANCE C. ORR
Press Representative	WILL ROSS
Stage Manager	T. DUKESON
Musical Director	W. L. MAIN
(For Thos. F. Convery's Enterprises, Ltd.)	

Please Order Early. Fill in this Slip
and hand to the Usher.

Seat No.   Row

Coffees

Teas

er Person,

ip when ordering ☞

BOOK YOUR PALACE THEATRE SEATS IN ADVANCE.

MARJORIE HAWKES

Ladies' Hairdresser

187a, NORTH RD., PRESTON
(2 minutes from Walker St.)

I am now open at the above address,
and old and new clients are assured of
my personal attention

Perms from 8/6 to £1-1-0

Telephone 3182

SEE PRESTON'S
FLOWER SHOW
EVERY DAY AT

HILL'S

ADELPHI STREET
PRESTON

Tel. 2347

J. COSTELLO

IS NOW ESTABLISHED AT

31 NEW HALL LANE, PRESTON

AS A COMPLETE BOYS' OUTFITTER

● EVERYTHING FOR YOUR BOY AT REASONABLE PRICES
● A SELECTION OF MEN'S WEAR ALWAYS IN STOCK

Bring your Insurance Prescription to

R. A. HILTON, M.P.S.

Dispensing and Photographic Chemist

Stockist of Patent Medicines, Baby Foods, Toilet Requisites. Complete stock of
pure drugs. Prescriptions accurately dispensed under personal supervision while
while you wait.
Twenty-four hour Printing and Developing Service

99 FISHERGATE HILL ——————— PRESTON
(At Bus Stop)

The Noted Tripe Shops in Preston
for the best quality TRIPE, SHEEP
FEET AND COWHEELS

W. CRANSHAW & Co.

Works: 64, Ribbleton Lane

Branches:
155 Friargate   225 North Road
57 Meadow Street   78 New Hall Lane
270 Fylde Road   25 Fylde Street
24 London Road   248 Ribbleton Lane

FRESH DELIVERIES DAILY

WHOLESALE & RETAIL CLOG
MANUFACTURERS
Men's and Youth's
Watertight Clogs
Boot and
Shoe
Repairs

ALSTON'S
129 LANCASTER RD., Preston
(2 mins. from the Covered Market)

Women's
& Children's
Strap or Clasp
Clogs

Men's Strong Working Boots

VISIT THE PALACE EVERY WEEK.

Two pages of advertisements from the Palace Theatre, Preston, in the 1940s.

THE PALACE REVUES AND VARIETY ARE BEST.

Tel. 4577

RADIO

HIS MASTER'S VOICE
BUSH
EKCO
PHILIPS, etc.

H. JONES M.I.R.E.
109 NEW HALL LANE
55 FRIARGATE : 69 RIBBLETON AVENUE

William GREEN

RAG & WOOLLEN MERCHANT

SKIN & METAL DEALER

BEST CASH PRICES

135 MARKET STREET
PRESTON. Tel. 2560

AFTER THE SHOW

CALL AT

JACKSON'S

CANNON STREET

FOR

HIGH-CLASS SUPPERS

AMERICAN MAGAZINE
SHOP

For Largest Selection of
AMERICAN MAGAZINES,
NEW & RARE BOOKS

visit

JACK MILLS

111 LANCASTER RD. (opp. Co-op.)
Your Magazines bought or exchanged

FOR

ELECTRICAL INSTALLATIONS

AND

RADIO SERVICE

C. HALLATT

135c, CHURCH STREET
(Near RITZ CINEMA)
Tel. 2486

HURRICANES! MESSERSCHMITTS!
SPITFIRES! HEINKELS!

Up to the minute
MODEL AIRCRAFT
Construction Kits
FROM

GEORGE EASTHAM

10 STANLEY ST., PRESTON

Balsa Wood and Model Accessories
Handicrafts and Hobbies supplies

STAYTITE COVER CO.

SPRINGFIELD MILLS, BROOK STREET, PRESTON
PHONE 2198

All Classes of WATERPROOF COVERS, TARPAULINS
and STACKSHEETS available for immediate delivery

LOWEST POSSIBLE PRICES — REPAIRS — RE-OILS — HIRE

REDUCED PRICES FOR MEMBERS OF H.M. FORCES.

The American Magazine Shop on Lancaster Road was a real sign of the times!

~ 149 ~

In aid of the Mayoress's Comforts Fund and Station Buffet

★

PALACE THEATRE, PRESTON

(By the courtesy of P. B. Broadhead & Sons)

★

ALL STAR

VARIETY MATINEE

Saturday, 9th December, 1939

at 2 p.m.

Our Grateful Thanks—

To Messrs. P. B. Broadhead & Sons for their generous loan of the Palace Theatre, together with Band, Staff and Lighting.

To the Blackpool Tower Co., Ltd., through whose courtesy the following artists are enabled kindly to give their famous acts : Rawicz and Landauer ; Norman Newman and his Band ; Doodles ; Sharp and Taylor; Cavalini's Canine Comedians.

To the Winter Gardens (Morecambe and Heysham) Ltd., for kind permission to present The Golden Voice of Melody, Les Allen, and his Two Pianists.

To other Artists who have so generously given their services.

To the Staff of the Palace Theatre, Ticket Sellers, and all who have contributed to the success of this effort.

THE GUARDIAN PRESS, FISHERGATE, PRESTON

Wartime Preston and this Palace Theatre programme says it all.

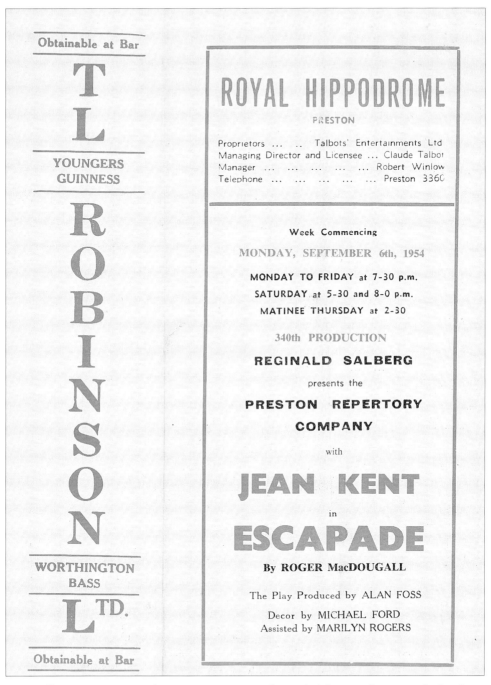

Obtainable at Bar

T L

YOUNGERS
GUINNESS

**R
O
B
I
N
S
O
N**

WORTHINGTON
BASS

L TD.

Obtainable at Bar

ROYAL HIPPODROME

PRESTON

Proprietors ... .. Talbots' Entertainments Ltd
Managing Director and Licensee ... Claude Talbot
Manager ... ... Robert Winlow
Telephone ... ... Preston 3360

Week Commencing

MONDAY, SEPTEMBER 6th, 1954

MONDAY TO FRIDAY at 7-30 p.m.
SATURDAY at 5-30 and 8-0 p.m.
MATINEE THURSDAY at 2-30

340th PRODUCTION

REGINALD SALBERG

presents the

**PRESTON REPERTORY
COMPANY**

with

JEAN KENT

in

ESCAPADE

By ROGER MacDOUGALL

The Play Produced by ALAN FOSS

Decor by MICHAEL FORD
Assisted by MARILYN ROGERS

Famous film star Jean Kent made a guest appearance in the 340th Salberg production, at the Royal Hippodrome in 1954.

1954—*THE DESERT SONG*
1955—*SHOW BOAT*

1956—*ANNIE GET YOUR GUN*
1957—*WILD VIOLETS*

THE
PRESTON MUSICAL COMEDY SOCIETY

PRESENTS

The Student Prince

A SPECTACULAR LIGHT OPERA

Book and Lyrics by DOROTHY DONNELLY

Music by SIGMUND ROMBERG

. at the .

EMPIRE THEATRE . PRESTON

MONDAY TO SATURDAY

4th to 9th May

1964

At 7-15 p.m.

Producer : HARRY CROSSLEY

1957—*BRIGADOON*
1958—*WHITE HORSE INN*
1959—*OKLAHOMA*
1960—*CAROUSEL*

1961—*THE KING AND I*
1962—*SOUTH PACIFIC*
1963—*THE LILAC DOMINO*

Affiliated to the National Operatic and Dramatic Association

The mothballed Empire Theatre saw one last full stage production in 1964.

The Merry Widow

President : Lt.-Col. RUDOLF ORD, M.B.E., J.P.

Under the Patronage of His Worship the Mayor of Preston and Members of the Corporation

Lt.-Col. RUDOLF ORD, M.B.E., J.P.

VICE-PRESIDENTS :

Julian Amery, Esq., M.P.
Mrs. Allison
R. Balmer, Esq., M.I.Mar.E.
Miss F. Bryning

Stanley Carwin, Esq.
Alan Green, Esq.
Alan Harrison, Esq., M.B.E.
Col. E. Robinson Hartley

Councillor Frank Hind
James Ingham, Esq.
R. Rhodes, Esq.
R. G. Thurnhill. Esq.

Neville Warburton, Esq.,
O.B.E., J.P.
Mrs. J. A. Wood, J.P.

PATRONS :

G. F. Baines, Esq.
G. E. Barnes, Esq.
J. F. Billinge. Esq.
T. C. Charnley, Esq.
W. F. Dawson, Esq.
J. Eyles. Esq.

T. R. Flintoff, Esq.,
M.B.E., J.P.
F. E. Howse. Esq.
Mrs. M. A. Leighton
J. Maddock. Esq.
W. Mercer. Esq.

T. C. Nicholson, Esq., J.P.
R. Robinson, Esq.
Miss M. A. Roscoe
Mrs. Rainford
W. Shorrock. Esq., M.B.E.
Miss M. Stopford

Miss J. Stewert
J. C. Turner, Esq.
L. B. Turner. Esq.
J. Walmsley, Esq.
E. D. White, Esq.

ASSOCIATES :

Mrs. G. Bradshaw
Mrs. P. Brady
G. H. Baines, Esq.
Mrs. L. Catterall
J. Coulthurst. Esq.
Miss O. Foden
R. Gray, Esq.

T. D. Hilton, Esq.
W. Hill, Esq.
R. M. Jamieson, Esq.
A. R. W. Jones, Esq.
Miss N. Marsden
S. Morrison, Esq.
Miss C. Parker

K. R. Parker, Esq.
Miss J. Patterson
W. E. Phillips, Esq.
T. Stanton. Esq.
Miss K. Slater
R. E. Strangeway. Esq.
I. Thomas, Esq.

Mrs. E. M. Tanner
Miss A. Winders
W. Whalley. Esq.
Mrs. H. Yates

The Queen's Hall was an unusual venue to be utilised by the resourceful members of the Preston Musical Comedy Society for a production of *The Merry Widow* in 1965.

ISMAIL
& Co. Ltd.

Wholesale
Tea and Coffee Merchants

Retail Shop:
**141a CHURCH STREET
PRESTON**

Telephone 54542

Wholesale:
**12-26 BACK LORD STREET
BLACKPOOL**

Telephone 23577 (2 lines)

HOTELS - CAFES - SNACK BARS
CANTEENS Etc. SUPPLIED

Our Reputation is Your Safeguard

D. T. JONES
The Modern Tailor
TO GENTLEMEN

READY-TO-WEAR DEPARTMENT

SPORTSWEAR, TWO-PIECE SUITS and RAINWEAR

LARGE SELECTION OF THE LATEST STYLES AND DESIGNS IN STOCK

Also at
123 Church Street
Blackpool

153 Friargate, Preston
Phone: 55468

Page Thirty

Two advertisements from *The Merry Widow* programme of 1965.